FROM MY INNER CHILD TO YOURS

NO ONE KNOWS ME

STELLA YANN

DISCLAIMER:

There are no names in this book for that's the way the story is intended to be delivered. If you recognise yourself or someone you know in the storyline, consider yourself lucky to be here: you've now become a teacher of life lessons on Earth.

STELLA YANN
NO ONE KNOWS ME: Inner Child Book

Paperback: The Inner Child Edition ISBN 978-1-0685737-0-5
Hardcover: The Dragon Edition ISBN 978-1-0685737-3-6
Hardcover: The Dragon Deluxe Edition ISBN 978-1-0685737-1-2
Ebook: The Alchemist's Guide ISBN 978-1-0685737-2-9

Published by Stellar Storytelling | stellarstorytelling.club
© 2024 by Stella Yann

MEET THE AUTHOR at **www.stellayann.com | hello@stellayann.com**

JOIN THE CONVERSATION on Instagram: **@noonebook | #noonebook**

To My Earth Family
THANK YOU

For my family I'd die
For my family I've already died
a thousand times or more

May the next generations
never repeat our life lessons
so they can have a childhood
without Ancestral trauma to heal

The Ancestors have found peace
It's time for us to do the same

To My Spirit Team
THANK YOU

This is not the book
I wanted to write

This book is a gift
from the Divine

Thank you for guiding me
through my Hero's journey
into my subconscious mind
and helping me become
a guide for others

a Lighthouse
a Lightworker

A Wayshower for
the New Earth

This book is for you
if you're ready to heal
and share your heart
with the world

I dedicate this book
to all the brave hearts
who choose to lead with love

TABLE OF CONTENT

To All Kickstarter Backers
THANK YOU

You believed in this project
before it was fully alchemised
into its final form and I owe you
my heartfelt gratitude:

Arn, Stacey, James,
Mihaela, Sonia, Shawna,
Michael, Hannah, Portia,
Lisa, Simona, Lilyana,
Desi, Issac, Karoline,
Sallie, Rachie, Sean,
Elizabeth, Amy, Joan,
Joanna, Jodie, Jennifer,
Jackie, Jess, Sadiq,
Maggie, Rennie, Peter

Thank you to my mentors too
May my Higher Self find yours
and gift you with abundance
for your continued support
across my many chapters
abroad and beyond

I'm home now

The 4 Elements of
ALCHEMY

The Universe is made up of Earth, Air, Water and Fire.

The Universe within you contains the same 4 elements and each element shapes your authentic personality.

This book will make use of the 4 elements:

AIR activates the Thinker! It's the element for one's Intellect, Information, Knowledge, Mindset and your Thoughts.

FIRE activates the Leader! It's the element for one's Passion, Purpose, Confidence and your Higher Self.

WATER activates the Healer! It's the element for one's Emotions, Connections, Empathy and your Feelings.

EARTH activates the Doer! It's the element for one's Identity, Integrity, Safety, Actions and your Habits.

Consider yourself an Alchemist from start to finish. You only need to remember you're the fifth element to activate the other four!

Part 1

TO BE YOURSELF

The
SHAME

"What's wrong with you?"

These 4 words shaped my existence on Earth for a very long time.

What was wrong with me?

Nothing. Nothing really.

I was just different – I was myself. My true self. Or at least I tried to be myself...

In a world that celebrates your ability to fit in, every time you stand out from the crowd with your true self and your authentic way of thinking, you're bound to be shamed for being different.

I was shamed for my differences and praised when I'd fit in and be a *"good sport"* or a *"good girl"*.

Being a *"good girl"* became a whole championship where the prize was more praise.

But every time I was praised for achieving something that I didn't care about, nor my Spirit was excited about, it was me who experienced the shame firsthand.

"Why did I listen to them?"

There was nothing wrong with me, of course. I knew it. On some level, they knew it too. And while they were too lost to recognise it consciously, I became more aware every day that I might lose myself even more if I continued to listen to them.

As the adults in the room roared victoriously with words of encouragement and praise for my achievements (and for listening to them), I carried the shame of betraying my true self, so that I could continue to be a good sport to the family, or the friendship, or the community...

Time went on and the list of people who expected me to behave in a certain way only ever increased. In fact, I was shamed even more harshly and more openly if I was to say something *"strange"*, *"bizarre"* or *"weird"*.

The memory of those 4 words echoed in my head from one season to the next one.

"What's wrong with you?"

And the more I matured and explored the world, the more my true self wanted to make an appearance with her strange, bizarre and weird ideas!

The Shame of BEING TOO MUCH

My first relationship started with this brief exchange:

"I hope I'm not going to be <u>too much</u> for you..."

My inner child finally said out loud what I'd been thinking about myself for almost 20 years of masking my true feelings.

The response?

"I fear I'm not going to be (good) enough for you..."

They say opposites attract and that's how two people with opposite personalities and opposite fears entered a union.

How long do you think the relationship lasted? It's longer than you think.

On the outside, we were perfect. On the inside, we knew what we had to go through on our own and as a team.

But that's the thing – we were never really a team.

For anyone watching us go through ups and downs as a couple, they could easily say: *"Those two were made for each other!"*

We were, indeed, made for each other – made to reflect each other's wounds, so that we can begin our trauma healing journey.

You see, our relationship was a trauma bond.

We weren't a team. We were bonded together by our shared shame of having experienced trauma as children and the key to healing was to recognise how each of us could teach the other something they never experienced in their own life.

Neither of us knew we had inner work to do at the time. We thought love was the answer and kept applying layers of *"I love you"* on top of every conversation that couldn't get to the heart of the issue.

As one might expect, the relationship did not work out.

We were young; we were mirrors who showed one another where the broken pieces were, yet we had opposite lessons to learn; we were on two different paths.

I had to learn how to apply more self-love because I was raised to give and give and give until there's nothing left to give.

He had to learn how to give without judgement and to pour into a chosen vessel without comparison or competition.

In the end, he could not claim me as his chosen one when there was much more to explore in the world and so I entered my self-love journey.

In other words, we could no longer learn side by side, so we had to part ways and that wasn't easy either, because the shame of letting go and failing and losing – even if what you got attached to was no longer <u>your favourite toy or person</u> – was too much to handle on top of the pre-existing shame.

We both had much to learn about accepting and receiving without shame, too.

We often end up prolonging our suffering, because we think of shame as the source of all experiences and over time we begin to believe in this false narrative so much that it becomes a guiding principle to choose *"the lesser evil"* versus our true happiness.

Maybe our first major relationship in life is supposed to be a trauma bond: to teach us patience and independence, to show us love and collaboration, to guide us back home to our true self.

In our case, we ended up torturing each other's Souls as we each tried to prove to the other that our fears were just that – fears.

A relationship that begins with fears will break apart because of those fears unless both individuals are willing to do the inner work to overcome them.

We both had a fear of being seen for who we truly were and deep down I know what was at the core of each of us – love. But there were many layers of authenticity that we each had to uncover, understand and feel comfortable with on our own before channelling that love into another human being.

Take away the shame of being yourself and all you're going to find are more reasons to celebrate being human, **just as you are**, regardless of your background story.

The Shame of **NOT BEING ENOUGH**

When our relationship ended, I remember thinking to myself:

"Love is not enough to save a relationship."

Many years have passed since the end of us as a couple and if I have to be honest, the love I once felt for this person is no longer there – energetically speaking.

I wish him well, and I have wished him well many times over the years, but I do not wish to repeat any more cycles of being misunderstood when all I ever wanted to do was to share my true Self with the world.

Maybe at the time I didn't know how to embody all of me, how to be myself in a society that wanted me to wear masks and perform, how to speak my truth without *losing my voice* during the heart-felt performance.

Yet, a part of me is certain that there was a point in our relationship when I was truly myself in all of my authentic glory – and that it was simply not good enough for this person.

He wanted me to continue to participate in the circus of life where humans were nothing but beasts who wore high street fashion labels and aspired to domesticate the rare breeds of the natural world as treasured pets and items they can use to gain more praise from peers.

But I was born to be wild.

Free.

Brave.

Honest.

Loyal.

I was a wild cheetah who wanted to roar with joy for having found love after many years of anticipation.

And somehow the wild cheetah in me ended up getting her prints devalued and mocked and even attacked by the animals with pack-mentality who only had 'BORN TO BE WILD' on their T-shirts: these were the animals who took pleasure in power plays and had no intention of ever being part of a community that promotes unity or growth or love.

They were too busy tearing each other apart.

A cheetah needs a partner who can keep up with her without trying to devalue her worth or bring her down to a lower level, so that he can feel more manly and in power.

A cheetah is not scared to walk alone when she has a legacy to protect.

My fear of not being enough did not last long for I had already spent plenty of time getting to the heart of who I am and I had found multiple aspects about my identity that were fascinating to explore.

But I did feel the fear of *not being good enough* recently and it arrived with a bang. Like a storm on a summer night as you're about to enjoy your slumber with the song of the birds. First arrives the lightning, then the thunder.

"What if you chose wrong? What if I'm not good enough?"

I found myself speaking directly to God as I realised my calling was much higher than I initially thought of it. My chest tightens as I write this – I still feel it, the fear of not being able to live up to the expectations of the Divine for my Soul may be limitless in other realms, but my vessel on Earth has limitations and I'm well aware of them by now.

Yet I was the first choice – the wild cheetah who was brave enough to walk away from people, places and packs that did not align with her true self.

A wild card in a game whose endgame was already predetermined.

Suddenly I was the wild, *weird*, hyper independent cheetah caught in the middle of a storm who had fear in her heart and God's voice in her ear: *"I believe in you."*

The Shame of **BEING DIFFERENT**

The shame of being yourself is really the shame of being different.

Isn't it amazing that we're all born to be different, yet the moment we realise it – we become so alienated from our own Nature, as if that realisation was never meant to be reached consciously!

"This is who I am."

This statement can be a double-edged sword. If it's applied into the conversation with the intention to stay true to one's authentic self, it is freeing and empowering. But if it's used to defend your Ego and the false reality you've built around enabling your coping mechanisms, because you're too scared to look within and face yourself in all of your Light and darkness – it becomes dangerous as it simultaneously blocks your growth and ruins your chance at building meaningful relationships.

The truth is we all have strengths and weaknesses.

Our strengths are the aspects of our identity that we have developed to the point of self-mastery over the years – they are the defining features of our character that make us who we are.

Our weaknesses, however, are the aspects of our true self that make us so special. They are what gives us more depth, flavour and room for growth, so that we can continue our personal evolution until our final breath.

When we meet someone who's fascinated by our perceived weaknesses – a person who allows us to drop down the masks, the protective layers and the heavy armour designed to hide our vulnerabilities – they become a safe harbour for us to continue our self-growth journey to the next level, where shame is simply the first step of the ladder.

In the meantime, the self-discovery journey gives you an opportunity to become that safe harbour for yourself: to be your own Lighthouse that holds space for the Light even in the darkest days or the loudest storms.

There's duality in all of us – you, me, our parents, friends we're yet to meet – that ensures true balance on Earth.

It's the yin-yang harmony set in motion!

Name **YOUR SHAME**

Let's bring in more details. The more specific you can get when describing your inner world, the more you'll be able to get to the heart of your SHAME and transform it into a growth opportunity.

Complete the following sentences to express what might have been suppressed for a long time:

SHAME OF BEING TOO MUCH
(e.g. energetic, hopeful, naive, strong, serious)

"I feel like I'm too much because I am ALWAYS…"

SHAME OF NOT BEING ENOUGH
(e.g. loving, affectionate, logical, fun, spontaneous)

"I don't feel good enough because I am NOT / I do NOT…"

SHAME OF BEING TOO DIFFERENT
(e.g. race, age, gender, features)

"I don't fit in because I am…"

Rise Above **YOUR SHAME**

Think of your life as a show that others are watching as you get to direct it and star in it. You're also the Chief Storyteller and you have just scheduled a press conference to release yourself from the bondages of your SHAME.

Let's report on what was the original state of your inner world and how you're going to be proceeding forward – this is your declaration of independence!

Pick one: **TOO MUCH | NOT ENOUGH | TOO DIFFERENT**

What's the story you're telling yourself?
Tip: Be as honest as possible with yourself
How can you rewrite the narrative?
Challenge: Write your own authenticity statement

Congratulations – you've just directed an episode of your life in a more conscious and empowering way!

Shall we examine GUILT next?

"What's wrong with you?"

"Nothing. I'm a wild cheetah born into a world of monkeys. You wouldn't get it…"

The

GUILT

Once you rise above the level of shame, get ready to experience the guilt of being yourself. If you're lucky, you will only have to face a couple of relatives who are under obligation to question your motives when you begin to mature and outgrow your previous coping mechanisms.

"How could you do that?"

How could you grow up? How could you answer back? How could you go against your own family? How could you support yourself or someone else more than you support your own blood? How could you skip a holiday or break free from tradition when family is everything?

The guilt-tripping doesn't happen all at once. It comes as a series of conversations and events that are meant to discourage you from abandoning your previous self, so that you can fit into the narrative of those around you a little bit longer.

When you choose to act like a version of yourself you've already outgrown, you are abandoning your future self that holds the blueprint to your true success in life.

Phase one of the guilt-tripping begins with a series of HOW-questions that target specific events and while every incident requires some of your energy to do damage control in your relationships by participating in the open discussion, what comes next is ten times heavier to handle:

"Why are you acting this way?"

This question arrives as a personal attack on your innermost self who has to face all of the triggers from the starting point of shame.

"Why am I like this? Maybe I am the problem..."

There's a reason GUILT and SHAME are the lowest possible frequencies we can experience in life – they paralyse us.

Guilt and shame block us from acting in alignment with our true self and bring us to a state of inner turmoil that slowly but surely guides us to self-destruct, so that we can remain in a cycle of toxic co-dependency with other adults who also haven't yet uncovered their true authentic self.

This explains why so many people on Earth are immature and insecure and unable to break free from the trauma bonds.

They are not learning the lessons required to mature their psyche, which would in turn help them outgrow their programming full of limiting beliefs that block their access to their limitless consciousness.

But what's worse – every year you remain in the toxic cycles of mind games and heartache, the armour you wear to protect your Inner Child gets heavier and more difficult to take off since now it's almost inseparable from your identity.

It's a paradox.

"Who am I without my coping mechanisms? Who am I without my trauma? Who am I when I let go of the fear?"

Many are scared to do the shadow work necessary to answer these questions and so they remain stuck in life, losing integral parts of themselves every day they remain plugged into a world matrix that continues to condition us all into blind submission to fit in with the norm and obey the rules.

I set myself free when I chose to trust my inner guidance wholeheartedly.

Some people I had to let go of, others I had to let down – I have no regrets.

In order to return back home to myself and give back to that inner child that was craving my attention all this time, I had to overcome my guilt that came as a result of wanting to grow and experience more of me and more of life as me.

The moment you forgive yourself for not knowing better and accept yourself as a person who is on a path of continuous evolution, no one will ever be able to get under your skin and attack your character from within.

But first – let's examine how guilt manifests in your inner world!

The Guilt of **BEING THE VICTIM**

Being the victim is easy. You kind of let it happen. You let yourself grow into a numb, mellow version of a human being who's half here and half in a state of dissociation.

Life happens to you and there's not much you can do about it but accept everything that comes your way: it's the victim's perspective of <u>surrendering</u>.

"There's nothing I can do."

Being the victim when you're overlooked and neglected is easy. You learn how to blend in, mind your business

and do what's necessary to survive in a world that has robbed you of your value.

Time passes and you're meant to advance your understanding of the world as well as your belonging in it, but you're still the same – a victim of your circumstances.

Your character is then shaped by an environment that couldn't care less about your individual needs as long as you participate in the mass culture structured around mass consumption of ideas, ideals and identification with the norm. Nothing more, nothing less.

There goes your authenticity. You know nothing about who you are and the society you're part of is happy to have you caged as a prisoner to the economy, because that means they have created another slave to the system.

But being the victim when someone's wronged you – that's a whole different story.

Why?

For one, you have a choice:

"Am I gonna allow my external circumstances to define my life, or am I gonna rise above them and act in alignment with who I am – and who I know myself to be, opposed to what has happened to me?"

Nothing reminds you of your free will quite like someone crossing your boundaries and going against you without any provocation.

I think this might be an "authenticity loop" in the Game of Life that occurs at a Divinely appointed time to shake our world and evoke our inner power.

When we are reminded of the brevity of our existence, we begin to cherish every day as the starting point of the next phase of our life.

What's more, we start to believe in our ability to channel our Inner Leader who can handle any challenge and save the day.

We are finally able to switch our mindset from:

"Why are bad things always happening to me? Why is it always me?"

To the glorious state of mind of:

"Why not me? Why not now? Why wait any longer to start anew!"

The Guilt of **BEING THE VILLAIN**

I have lived for so long I can almost remember all the times I died and returned as a new version of myself – each time even more authentic and honest than before.

When did I become the villain of the story?

Every time I had to let go of a connection that would keep me barely standing on my Phoenix's ashy bones that awaited my acceptance that it's over.

"Let go," the Spirit of the Phoenix would whisper to me. *"Let go. You did everything you could. You completed your mission. It's time to rest now. Take a deep breath and let it all burn away... we will meet you on the other side."*

Who was this magical "we"? My Spirit Team, of course, that has been protecting me and guiding me since day 1.

There are big energetic shifts that happen in the spiritual world that go beyond our understanding and every time a connection ends in the physical world, it sets a chain of events in motion that will help everyone involved continue their personal evolution.

Unfortunately, I am one of the change agents that have been embedded into the Game of Life without warning or instructions.

A wild card!

I had to figure it out all on my own – that my presence triggers people: into healing, into awakening, into ascension, into facing their Shadow Self.

I may be healing and a source of Divine love, peace and wisdom, but I am also a Wayshower, which means I don't mind disrupting the status quo if there's a better way to do things. I am the way through the power of my Divine guidance. A vessel that's sharing the messages and leading the way to the best of my abilities at any given moment.

I do not claim I know everything. What I'm saying is that the guidance that comes from within will always be the main priority as to how I live my life because I have committed myself to my purpose – and to the Divine.

What does that mean for my Human Self? Well, I experienced the same trauma and conditioning like everyone else, but I managed to override the programming time and time again until I fully ascended to the level where I can channel my Higher Self freely and achieve full alignment with my purpose.

There are actions I'm not proud of, like everyone else on Earth.

There are days I lose access to my higher guidance, like everyone else on Earth.

There are people I miss with all of my heart – people I could never return to because they are not part of the timelines I'm meant to reach, so that I can accomplish my higher calling on Earth.

There are moments when I feel like an ordinary human and then I remember…

I answered the call.

I said "Yes" to my higher purpose on Earth and there's no going back to the life, or versions of life, I shared with the people who came before my calling.

Speaking of calls…

Yes, I had to break up with someone over a phone call.

Yes, I had to leave a job over another phone call.

Yes, I had to deny a lot of phone calls, delete many of my accounts and disappear from multiple connections.

Yes, I had to go through seasons where people thought I was acting beyond weird, that I had perhaps gone crazy, because my behaviour no longer made sense to their understanding of the world and where they had placed me in that world.

Yet my life always went into unpredictable directions, even before I started walking on my spiritual path. A life that had me change 10 different apartments in 10 years across 3 different countries. No place I could call home, because just as I was about to settle down, the next big shift in my life would begin…

Yes, I have a big heart – a heart that can make room for everyone – but eventually my Soul became exhausted from dragging everyone I knew on adventures that were meant just for me, so that I can learn the lessons required of me to become the person who can handle the calling placed on my life.

I don't owe those that I've left behind an explanation, because this calling is much bigger than anything you can imagine. Nonetheless, I would like to say *"I'm sorry"* for leaving so abruptly from your life if you happen to pick up this book and read it on your own self-growth journey.

Leaving you was never a move on some imaginary chess board.

Leaving you along with leaving so many things behind was part of the sacrifice one must make when they are ready to serve humanity.

Leaving you was personal, the most personal thing I've ever done.

Because every time I left someone, I also left a version of me that could not come further on the journey forward.

Leaving was the bravest thing I had to learn on my ascension journey or I'd never been able to step into my authenticity.

It was my declaration that I am ready to be the person I came onto Earth to be!

The Guilt of **BEING YOURSELF**

After what you've read about me so far, you might consider me a self-aware person.

My self-awareness helped me rise above my circumstances when I had to deal with challenges that required a lot of strength.

I had the opportunity to spend a year in Italy as part of my university programme and something told me to take it. Unfortunately, at some point I got really sick and for the first time I had to face a challenge I was not adequately equipped for: I had to go to a doctor to get some antibiotics without fully speaking the language. Oh, and I was barely able to move or talk, because I was so, so *physically* tired.

To this day I'm not sure how I summoned the strength to actually leave the bed and take the steps, one foot in front of the other, to the middle aged specialist that smelled of orange and mint and had no clue what I was trying to say beyond my broken Italian accent and my throbbing sinuses that were somehow clearing the way for me to see things from the right perspective.

"How did I end up here? What pushed me this far to the edge? When did I give up on life to the point of being so sick that I'm falling apart?"

I was not being harsh on myself, I was finally facing the truth. Something had to change and the change had to start with finding out when I lost my spark for exploring, learning and writing – because even before I got sick, I felt depressed and without much inspiration to do anything.

My stubbornness was a useful feature, but I realised it had led me to take part in battles that were never mine to begin with. It had fueled a fire in me that was channelled in all the wrong pursuits – until I had a word with the Phoenix Spirit who guided me through every failed attempt at loving myself, so I can course-correct.

A year later I was living in Scotland and I got sick out of the blue – I had to enter the hospital for the very first time in my life.

I remember I woke up around 5AM in the morning and I just knew, *"This is serious. We need to go to the hospital now."*

My inner guidance was with me as always and even though I was scared for my life, I knew better than to doubt and so I kept moving forward one step at a time.

It turned out to be kidney infection due to a kidney stone that had blocked the passage to my bladder and if I had not taken it seriously and acted so quickly, my kidney might have erupted and caused major internal damage with fatal consequences.

I had an emergency surgery the next day and the inflammation to my body was so strong, I had to stay in the hospital for an extra week, because my fever would not subside as I was allowing myself to finally be taken care of and rest.

Do you know what these two stories share in common?

The same romantic partner who tortured my heart so much, I actually chose to self-destruct myself in order to stay with him a little bit longer.

How long do you think it took me to figure it out? A lot longer than I should have. Or maybe I did figure it out straightway, I just didn't want it to be true.

There's great wisdom in understanding that sometimes you have to be the villain in someone else's story in order to accomplish your purpose on Earth – there's nothing more dangerous to your health than going against your own intuition.

If you lose yourself, what good is your sacrifice to love someone else to the point of total collapse?

Where's the honour in showering someone else with your love when your own heart and body are aching due to the lack of love you have for yourself?

This is what I mean when I say there's great wisdom in knowing when to leave a person or a situation.

If I could turn back time, would I do it again?

Probably. Maybe. I don't know.

It's easy to review our failed attempts in life with judgement and guilt, but the biggest lesson remains the experience.

Without the experience, how can you truly know what love is and how magnificent love feels and how love shouldn't really hurt you so much to the point of leaving you in the hospital.

I wonder sometimes, what my life would have been if my threshold for pain wasn't so high from childhood – would I have been able to pick up on the signs that some relationships were not really kind to my heart, but rather a challenge as to how much pain I can handle before I collapse or lose myself entirely?

But I suppose there's a reason the events in my life have happened in this order.

Now I know what it feels like to love myself wholeheartedly and to accept myself just as I am. It's only taken leaving everyone else behind, because they were not ready to handle my fragile heart and my big calling on Earth!

Rewrite **YOUR GUILT**

Before you can integrate all parts of yourself, it's essential that you become aware of them. This exercise will help you recognise outdated aspects of your identity that you're ready to transform!

Complete the following sentences to let go of what might have been holding you back for a long time:

GUILT OF BEING THE VICTIM
(e.g. lack of boundaries, keeping the peace, ignoring your needs)

"I act(ed) like the VICTIM when..."

GUILT OF BEING THE VILLAIN
(e.g. setting boundaries, sharing your truth, honouring your needs)

"I am / became the VILLAIN when..."

GUILT OF BEING YOURSELF
(e.g. different beliefs, healthy habits in a dysfunctional environment)

"It hurts or feels heavy to be ME when..."

Rise Above **YOUR GUILT**

Guilt keeps you chained to the past – energetically speaking. If you're ready to free yourself from the bondages that have caused enough scar tissue on your heart, let's consider how your actions can shift your perspective and vice versa.

Let's examine how guilt manifests in your own relationships and how you can finetune your inner wiring to welcome new energy and the new opportunities that come with it!

Pick one: **TOO MUCH | NOT ENOUGH | TOO DIFFERENT**

What's your default behaviour when networking?
Tip: Ask people how they viewed you when you first met
How can you act instead? What about your attitude?
Challenge: Write your purpose-driven networking introduction

Well done – you've taken another step on your healing journey to unlocking more of your potential.

What's next? We take a deep dive into GRIEF!

"Why are you acting this way?"

"Darling, I'm a Wayshower! Ask the Phoenix..."

Part 2
TO LOSE YOURSELF

The
GRIEF

When you get lost in life, you're usually the last person to figure it out.

People around you see the spark in your eyes slowly dim down and disappear, but they don't quite know what to make of it, because they've seen it time and time again in society.

<u>The dreamers</u> who want to change the world sooner or later begin to tone down their messages and lose their enthusiasm for progress, because no one else can hear the drums that are guiding them to dance with joy, passion and optimism as the rest of society is stuck in the monotony of life.

It's hard work being a dreamer, because the work you're doing is energetically charged, and when you have so much negativity and even apathy coming from your environment, it takes a truly resilient Light to keep shining in the darkest of times.

Most dreamers never quite become the positive change makers (or Lightworkers) they envision themselves to be, because they lose their inner Light – or get lost in the Light as they refuse to acknowledge the Dark as part of the duality.

In order to generate enough Light to trigger a spark in the system and change it, you have to be willing to burn down in the name of the cause you're fueling with your bright Spirit – this is the Phoenix Spirit in action.

Most dreamers cannot handle the pivotal moment known as their breakthrough. They give up at the point of their breakdown, which is precisely the opening into their future that channels more of their purpose from potential energy into kinetic energy.

Some refer to this process as manifestation: those that actually understand what it means to manifest in alignment with your Higher Self.

Others might call it alchemy: in order for you to accomplish something new, you must first give up something old – the Law of Duality is at play here, but also the idea that you cannot create something out of nothing. You must be willing to surrender the version of life that no longer serves you, so that you can ascend to a version of higher meaning, higher purpose and higher belonging.

Working with the Law of Attraction – and manifesting – is not about surrounding yourself with crystals and praying to the Gods for material abundance while frantically pointing to your vision board.

That's your Ego wanting for you to continue to look after it at the expense of your spiritual growth!

Your Ego is very skilled at using emotional resources to keep you tied to versions of yourself that are not healthy for your evolution – versions that are attached to the pain and the trauma and the narratives built around conditional beliefs that rob you of your power to be a limitless Creator on Earth.

Manifesting is about channelling your potential in a way that allows you to make your inner child's dreams come true as you plug into the natural matrix on Earth and contribute to the wellbeing of all of humanity.

To become this Master Manifestor that's respected by both your neighbours on Earth and your Guardian Angels above Earth requires resilience of Spirit and a pure heart that will 100% be tested through a series of obstacles in the name of Love.

"Are you willing to believe in love after everything you've gone through?"

That's the test.

The Divine tests all of us while we are on Earth to determine if we have the right heart posture to handle a bigger calling.

If we do not, there's another matrix that is continuously recruiting Souls who are unwilling to do the inner work necessary to become greater versions of themselves: they become slaves to the system and manifest on behalf of the system, never quite sure of themselves and their place on Earth, because they have willingly disconnected from their true authenticity and true calling.

"Get someone else to do it!"

That's their answer.

They refuse to answer the calling – they would much rather enjoy their Earthly experience and ignore the consequences of their actions.

Since we are all interconnected on Earth, we are always surrounded by groups of people who either belong to the Lightworkers that are willing to do the inner work, or by the Beneficiary Bystanders that do not really care about what happens around them so long as they are doing well.

That's where things get tricky!

People get paired up in friendships and romantic relationships only to eventually come to the realisation that their partner is *"nothing like them"*.

This is one of the tests – do you remain in this connection trying to *"fix" or "save" or "lead"* the other person to a place of wisdom and healing and growth, or do you let go of the mis-match, so that you can align with a better match?

You cannot do the inner work on behalf of someone else. You can only do the inner work for yourself.

Any attempts to heal, teach or grow someone else will be futile; unless they are your child, in which case you are to guide them as part of your mission on Earth.

The grief enters the storyline when we remain in connections that are not a match to who we are, because we really, really want them to be something they're not.

The grief is above all about losing ourselves in these connections.

We enter relationships with a clear understanding of who we are – we are like the finished Lego set. But by the end of a mis-matched relationship or friendship, we are broken down into individual tiny pieces that we are then tasked with picking up without any instructions or help from the outside world.

Why? Because it's our mess.

Remember that you were the person who wanted to be loved so much, you chose to stay in a connection that never truly saw your value, your Light and your presence – or worse, they chose to ignore it, neglect or belittle it.

No one is responsible for fixing your mess, the mess you create by choosing at random or choosing for the sake of making a choice, without first being truly connected to your innermost self.

What we grieve in life is not the people we've lost, but the way they reflected back onto us our own brilliance – our own Light.

The more you give up on yourself, the more you will seek validation from others and the more you will suffer because of it.

Relationships are meant to be about sharing our Light with each other, so that we can reflect back onto one another how much we shine on our own and as a team. In the process, we also help each other illuminate aspects of ourselves that might have been hidden or completely forgotten about.

We need one another, but only when there's a mutual desire to grow side by side.

The Grief of GETTING PICKED LAST

Have you ever been picked last? Wait, let me rephrase the question.

Have you ever been in a relationship with someone who always picked you last?

I'm talking about…

- A friend who would cater to the needs of everyone else before you
- A parent who would praise the gifts of everyone else before you
- A life partner who would listen to the advice of everyone else before you

Getting picked last sucks, especially when it's coming from people that we consider our closest friends, family and tribe members.

I was never a *"Pick me!"* girl and maybe that's why I ended up getting picked last in many settings, from my social circle through school and work opportunities.

Instead, I was the reasonable girl who had the ability to maintain her positive state of mind whatever happened – heartbreak, grief, disappointment, neglect, maybe even abuse.

"Pick me!"-people love the attention, the suspension amidst the competition and the thrill of having been selected before others, even if that adrenaline-filled space only lasts a couple of moments.

I don't care much about being picked first, so long as I'm picked for the right things. And to be honest, I don't think I care much about being picked last either. Maybe I get to be the final person on a team who's missing a creative spirit or someone who can offer intuitive insights – the missing puzzle piece, right?

But the grief of being picked last in relationships where people took time to get you to trust them and got you to suspend your walls, so that you can expose your true vulnerabilities in front of them... that's the grief of being manipulated.

Emotional manipulation can happen at any point of your journey. It's much trickier to navigate and understand than traditional manipulation that is based on mind games that mainly have to do with questioning your logical abilities *(so that you get activated or triggered to prove yourself through doing what the person needed you to do in the first place)*.

Emotional manipulation is a lot more intentional. It's personal. You are personally chosen to be the target of manipulation, yet you're not special to the manipulator whose only purpose is to feel superior to you. In fact, the only reason they chose you is because you showed them an aspect of yourself that made them feel inferior to you – that's why they picked you as one of their targets with the goal to diminish some of your shine and confidence, so that they can restore their image of being superior to you (within their own mind and hopefully to the rest of the world).

The grief of getting picked last by the people you love the most is really the grief that comes from the realisation that they never really cared about you the way that they made you believe that they did.

Maybe they never even got to meet who you truly are, because they were mostly dealing with their own internal compass of what were the qualities you displayed that needed *"toning down"* or some sort of adjustment, so that the false balance within their dysfunctional status quo can be maintained.

Don't get it twisted. This is personal, but it has everything to do with the one who's doing the manipulating.

The people who manipulate others on an emotional level are simply lost Souls who have not figured out who they are and when they see someone who's certain about their identity, *they feel personally attacked* because you are serving as a BIG FAT MIRROR to all of their questions, doubts, fears and insecurities.

Your presence forces them to have no other choice but to look into the mirror and finally face themselves. What they'll see staring back at them is their own wounded Ego and their shattered inner world due to the trauma they are yet to heal.

This is the starting point of one's healing journey for most people, especially those who have arrived on Earth in toxic dysfunctional families.

You did nothing wrong. In fact, you played the part you needed to play in their life, so that they can continue their self-discovery journey on a deeper level.

The Grief of **NEVER GETTING PICKED**

Let's talk about unrequited love.

What do you imagine when you hear these two words – "unrequited love"?

Jane Austin, forbidden love, friendship zone, less than desirable, it's complicated, hidden feelings, one-sided relationship, and the list goes on.

To me, unrequited love is about putting up with what you were given. My Spirit grew up around people – friends and family – who put up with me as *"the gift"* that was different and occasionally difficult, *yet somehow they found a way to love it.*

Parents don't pick their children, but I have a sneaky feeling that children pick their parents from the Astral realm before they arrive and so I was the wild card of a child that chose a family that had no clue what was about to enter their lives. I was quiet, but different – and that was precisely what set me apart from the rest of the pack from the very beginning of my journey in this avatar.

Maybe I was myself, my authentic self from the get-go, even when it felt like I could be even more of myself – never quite giving into the temptation to be like everyone else, mostly because I couldn't.

There have been so many times on my journey, more times than you could imagine, where I have spoken directly to God – *"Why can't I be normal?"* – knowing exactly what I'm asking for: to be less of myself.

It's not that I didn't love myself, I honour and treasure every atom of my existence, but I knew my encoding was too complicated for most people to interact with and understand[1].

What I was asking was, *"Could you make me easier to understand for others?"*

---

[1] **The Starseed wiring** – something I'll explore in my next book

The Divine would laugh in my ears, saying things like *"You were made for times that haven't yet arrived – have patience, dear Child"* or *"One day you'll see why you had to be delivered on Earth the way that you are."*

I realise now I had to learn how to dim down my Light and regulate how much of me I showcase into interactions from a young age, which is something no child should go through.

Children should be able to enjoy their childhood years without having to worry about the reactions of their parents or teachers simply because they are not capable of speaking the same Soul language.

Children need a safe space to explore and express themselves. I didn't get that, so I created it for myself, but in the meantime there were definitely attempts to be more like the rest of the pack, because really I was just another Soul on Earth who sought to find belonging amidst her quest for higher meaning; yet every time my purpose took priority.

There were ideas that wanted to be explored, questions that demanded to be asked, opinions that needed to be expressed. I was merely the channeler: the vessel that offered my consciousness a space to explore all of it.

My grief of never getting picked by my friends and family never lasted for too long, since I knew deep down that I chose them and that the lessons we learned together would make for valuable research that will positively impact all of humanity.

As one of the Wild Cards in the Game of Life, I had to disrupt the status quo as a *"glitch"* in the system, so that the new could be infused into the old and I had to do it in a way that allowed me to still be part of the old structures in order for it to be successful.

Did I know what I was doing at the time? No. I simply sought to be myself and get to the heart of what it means to be human. What *"gave me away"* was my thirst for higher meaning and the fact that when things didn't make sense, I would question them and have the courage to pursue the answers.

To my environment, I felt like a burden – a nuisance. And when they tried to get me to be like everyone else, they became a burden to me – a nuisance.

Authenticity seeks authenticity in the same way people operating in the comfort zone of familiarity seek more of the familiarity that gives them a sense of peace, even if it's false peace, so that we can each continue building our own legacy.

Life's not easy, but the Souls I met on my journey all made it easier, because every connection taught me something valuable about myself and what it means to be human.

I did love everyone on my path regardless and while it hurt me that I couldn't be more of service to them, I knew they couldn't be more of service to me either: we were no longer in alignment with our inner wiring past a certain point and nothing could ever change that.

We were on two separate life missions: one was about building a community in the familiar grounds based on familiar knowledge, the other one was about bringing new energy on Earth directly from the Ether of all living beings and channelling ancient wisdom that came from Ancestors whose ideas got buried under the layers of conformity that somehow passed the test of time.

When we didn't think too much about the fine print and allowed ourselves to just be who we are, we could find moments of appreciation for our differences and get lost in the present moment until we were called back to our assignments.

Here's a rule for the general public, regardless of their age: one can never erase or rise above the Laws of the Universe, whether they remember them or not. The Laws of the Universe govern anything in existence on Earth and beyond.

I was operating under the Laws of the Universe as one of the Divine Messengers on a divine assignment – and, of course, I remembered nothing of it until I turned 30.

The Grief of **PICKING YOURSELF**

When the Universe tells you to *"Let go"*, do you trust it?

"Let go now. It's OK to let go now. You're safe. You're loved. You're protected."

Against all odds, I let go of everything: everything that attached me to my old life.

No one knew I was capable of doing it: picking myself.

No one knew it cannot be undone or reversed: my old conditioning was gone.

No one knew what's to come next: myself included.

The instructions didn't go beyond *"Let go"*.

So I let go of the old social media accounts: one by one, I erased the presence of my old Self (the one who naively gave people chance after chance).

I let go of the old connections that once filled my Soul: friendships that no longer knew who I was and friendships that maybe *never knew* who I was.

I let go of the old tasks that previously kept me up channelling my potential past midnight: I knew I had more to give, *I always do*, but calling back my energy from everything that wasn't 100% me meant that I could then invest my energy into everything that was.

I let go of the old stories about who I am and who I'm not: this was a blank canvas and I was given all the colours to work with, so why would I stick to a black and white version when I could add plenty of spark to my authenticity?

I let go of the old beliefs passed down onto me from family and friends: the healing happened in waves, and each time another layer of false conditioning was removed, I felt lighter, like I could flow with more ease in this grand dance with the Universe.

I let go of the old traditions that once united my people, because quite frankly I didn't even know who my people were anymore…

Did I have anyone in my corner? Anyone who understood me or my journey? Even one person who was ready for and capable of holding space for me to be myself?

Honestly, no.

But I could see a whole tribe of people on their way – my true soul tribe. I could hear them in the distance as my spiritual sight was getting activated along with my psychic gifts and I knew I'd be OK.

I let go of everything and everyone familiar amidst the most profound transformation of my life and I had no one but myself to count on to make it through the storm. One foot in front of the other, I kept walking through the valley of shadows.

At first I couldn't see the Light, darkness enveloping all of me. But then it dawned on me that I was the Light, that it was my inner guidance that represented the Light within the darkness.

Eventually I made it out of the storm – and walked right into another storm. The most transformative seasons of our life arrive with a series of storms: not without bruises or aches, but with a renewed sense of trust in one's Self.

That was the lesson all along – you pick yourself not to prove to the rest of the world that you are worthy, but because you've finally understood it yourself.

No one prepares you for the grief of picking yourself.

When you grieve the loss of someone, you have friends and family to help you with your pain.

But when you pick yourself as a response to everyone in your life trying to reduce you to a version they could handle and feel comfortable with – there is no one to help you hold the pain.

You hold onto that pain on your own as a way to honour your Inner Child and show them the kind of love they never experienced throughout your entire life.

A love that doesn't seek to change you but tries to celebrate you in all of your ups and downs: true unconditional love.

No one knew my pain the way no one knew me: no one but the Divine. They were with me every step of the journey and this is the only reason I am still here.

The love the Divine has shown me has given me the strength to carry on in the biggest storms and the faith to believe in myself when I almost lost all of my Light in the darkness.

To say I did it on my own would be a lie, but if someone actually took the time to observe me as I danced my way around the world, they would testify: *"She did it on her own"*.

Reframe **YOUR GRIEF**

In order for you to shed your old skins and masks, you must first acknowledge that you're wearing them. Let's explore your grief together.

Complete the following sentences to take off parts of the armour that has been weighing you down for a long time:

> **GRIEF OF GETTING PICKED LAST**
> (e.g. for partnership, for promotions, for advice)

"I am / was always the last choice for…"

> **GRIEF OF NEVER GETTING PICKED**
> (e.g. in society, in competitions, in career journey)

"I am / was never the one to be picked or seen for my…"

> **GRIEF OF PICKING YOURSELF**
> (e.g. dating patterns, family dynamics, work boundaries)

"I had to learn to pick myself when it comes to…"

Alchemise **YOUR GRIEF**

Grief blocks your ability to alchemise your pain into passion and creations that allow you to channel your potential. If you're ready to rewrite your story and remove the blockages, this exercise will help you embody more of your limitless Inner Creator.

Let's connect the dots between your existing superpowers and your new beginning by purging some of the grief that is no longer a viable source of life!

Pick one: **(NEVER) GETTING PICKED (LAST) | PICKING YOURSELF**

Who are you when you wait for others to pick you?

Tip: Consider how your sense of identity has changed over the years

How does it feel to release yourself from expectations?

Challenge: Write a loving self-affirming statement

You'll get bonus points if you take a moment to write a short letter to your Inner Child starting with **"I am here now. Let's…"**.

Our healing journey continues with ANGER. Ready?

"What happened to you?"

"Life. It's a spectrum. Some days it feels sunny and on others it gets really dark. It's been dark for a while..."

The

ANGER

If grief comes in waves, so does anger. But if grief paralyses you, anger activates something primal in you that gets you to move and act!

Anger has helped me channel my energy to manifest quantum jumps in ways that *my optimism could never* – and while I am well aware of this, I still prefer to use my positive energy to direct my life.

Sometimes, however, we need to tap into our darkness in order to move beyond all the levels, chapters and lessons that are no longer serving our growth.

I still remember the moment someone ignited a spark in me that allowed me to manifest not one but two job opportunities that would later define my career path in major ways.

It all happened one afternoon in the middle of nothing.

I received a call from my future-to-be boss. We had agreed that I'd start working there after my notice period which was extended by a week.

Yet he still asked me, *"So you're coming tomorrow?"*

To which I replied kindly and calmly, *"No. We agreed I'd start a week later, which means I'll be in next Monday."*

He grunted, mumbled something to himself, replied OK and then hung up on me.

I put down the phone and the thought flashed in my mind as clear as ever:

"No one… speaks to me… this way."

In a matter of seconds, I was already browsing other available jobs.

That evening I applied to five positions at five companies.

The first one ignored me.

The second one gave me a call but we both realised it wasn't a match.

The third one invited me for an interview and despite my best intentions, I knew my heart wasn't in it.

The fourth one invited me for an interview and took the time to introduce me to the team and the company processes before we parted ways with a big smile on our faces and joy in the heart. Later in the day they offered me the role – which was queued to be the role I'd begin in less than two months.

In the meantime, I began my job with my grumpy boss a week after the call.

He wasn't grumpy towards me, as it turned out – he was just grumpy with life. The problem was that as soon as I stepped into the building, I knew…

"Oh, I need to quit this job."

It took me about 3 weeks to quit. I knew from the moment I stepped into the building that this wasn't going to be the role for me, yet I gave it a shot – I wasn't going to quit from day 1, after all.

Now I know it's OK to quit things when they don't feel in alignment with your true self or true values: sometimes it really is a matter of minutes before you can tell, other times it takes years – or until we learn how to be honest with ourselves without judgement for our true needs.

You might ask, *"Well, didn't you know where the job was going to be?"*

No, the interview took place in a fancy new building at a completely different location. The actual job was in a single room within a huge, post-communist building that had almost no life in it, a refuge to people who were conditioned to submit to a life of routines and follow orders between their coffee breaks.

I wanted to change the world. I had dreams that I wasn't willing to abandon just yet, *even if a part of me felt defeated and abandoned at the time.*

My anger subsided as soon as I completed my application spree that one afternoon, but this uneasy feeling that <u>I wasn't where I was supposed to be</u> lingered until I handed in my notice after 3 weeks and peace washed over me instantly.

What happened with the fifth position that I applied to?

They actually flew me over for an interview a couple of weeks after I'd started at the fourth company – and that was the role that I'll forever treasure as my biggest creative bootcamp. A role that was made for me. A role that defined my career path for good. A role that brought me back home to myself. A role that I considered for a very long time *"my saving grace"* for it breathed new life in me after I had lost my spark in a very, very disappointing relationship that nearly destroyed my Spirit.

Who knows – maybe it was the job that breathed life into me (the people, the location, the move abroad) or perhaps I breathed new life into myself by being the brave traveller, creative communicator and enthusiastic change maker I always knew myself capable of becoming!

As one of my mentors said at the time, *"You did the work, I simply reminded you that you were capable of doing it."*

The Anger of **LOSING YOUR WAY**

It's funny to talk about anger when anger is one of my non-states. According to my human design profile, it is the aspect of who I am that is least definitive of me.

I am a peacemaker. A quiet messenger of creative, sometimes bold ideas that likes to mind her business, research and observe in solitude, and write stuff about what it means to be human.

You might know the type – introvert, INFJ, empath.

For me to get angry requires a lot of patience with someone who after numerous attempts finally crossed the threshold of my boundaries – and I have a huge pain threshold.

If you don't believe me, ask my dermatologist: she has repeatedly burned my face with one of the strongest lasers in the world to melt away the scars that once defined my comfort zone. Now they're just constellations that remind me of my strength, imagination and ability to be gentle even in a time of adversity.

I guess I was angry when I was a teenager that there was no one around me that could just *"get me"*.

Unfortunately, that feeling remained all throughout my life. Fortunately, since the feeling of being a stranger among friends and family had become the norm, I found a way to befriend myself, which made my journey a lot easier as I travelled the world like a free atom in a system that polarised the elements to stick to each other.

I guess I was angry when I *"lost my face"* after getting my whole body inflamed, which forced me to go through many seasons of serious acne that in hindsight helped me find my way to literature and creative writing, which then allowed me to channel the pain into words of inspiration for others.

Every misfortune has a silver lining. At the time I couldn't grasp it, since I couldn't face the mirror or even hug people, because there were days when every part of my body was so inflamed it hurt me to even be touched.

Now I understand that my consciousness was expanding through the experience of pain, or you know, I can alchemise the story by putting a creative spin on it.

I guess I was angry when I called the love of my life and he replied *"Hello, my love"* thinking that I was someone else and yet I didn't hang up the phone, but pretended like this was just some big misunderstanding – and then stayed in the relationship for another 3 years.

I guess I was angry when I went to live in Italy and instead of enjoying the culture, the language and the people – I found myself depressed because love had turned me from a free abundant atom into a foreign polarised element that couldn't function properly without her other half. Sure, it was codependency, a nasty one at that, but everyone else had someone, so why couldn't I hold onto the dream fever a little bit longer? So I did.

I guess I was angry when I finally figured out that I had lost my way and there was no one but me to hold responsible for it – and so I had to learn accountability as the way to return to myself.

But first, I had *more losing to do* and more anger to experience as I watched my whole life turn into a series of dissolving relationships that left bitterness in me after years of dancing and singing and drinking beside each other.

The Anger of **LOSING YOUR PEOPLE**

If people could never *"get you"*, were they really your people?

There weren't many people I wanted to hold dear to me and bring them along with me wherever I went, but at some point even the few individuals that I had placed firmly in my heart became too heavy to carry.

For one, I couldn't really share everything that was happening in my life – there were so many stories from so many remote parts of the world that just weren't a match to the daily experiences of those whose home was far away from mine. It was the little details that mattered the most, yet those details couldn't really fit in the flow of updates in the group chats or Zoom calls that attempted to save connections that were never meant to be a rescue mission.

We were moving in different directions and cared about different things that had us abandon a part of our true selves in order to participate in the old dynamics. I was among the first ones to let go, but we all knew the time was coming.

After having been raised in a household where adults constantly left, I learned the hard way to appreciate when people were around and let them be when they were away.

Was I angry to be left behind? Sure. Did I make peace with it? I had to.

Did I become the person who leaves people behind? Possibly. Was it a decision I made consciously to make up for my years of abandonment? No, not really.

A lot of my life decisions have been guided by my inner compass. If I had a *"good feeling"* about something or someone, I opened up to them. But if I sensed that it wasn't safe for me to be myself, I closed off just as quickly.

My inner compass made it possible for me to make huge leaps of faith in life, but it also made it impossible for me to participate in relationships that I had outgrown for a variety of reasons. And since I changed a lot faster than most people, I outgrew relationships faster than most people too.

This was one of the reasons I was angry for being alone and misunderstood in the world. As soon as I found someone that I could relate to and share the journey of life with, I'd almost certainly *"outgrow"* them in a matter of months – mostly, due to who I was and not something that they did.

My wiring is all about self-growth and channelling more of my potential.

Most people are not interested in growth the way that I am and it's taken me a lot of years to make peace with that fact. It's also taken me a lot of courage to be honest with myself around the types of changes, sacrifices and compromises that I'm willing to make when it comes to self-growth.

I once abandoned myself and my wiring for self-growth, because I wanted to stay within a dynamic that allowed me to experience a slice of love. This choice nearly destroyed me, because it went against my true authentic self.

So losing my people might sting a little bit, but it doesn't compare to the pain and devastation that comes from losing yourself.

The Anger of **LOSING YOURSELF**

The worst devastation one could ever experience is not the loss of property, the loss of income, or even the loss of someone you love – it's the loss of your own Self.

To love someone as yourself and to love someone as the shadow of yourself are two completely different things.

We grieve when we lose people we love and when we don't get an opportunity that was a right fit to who we are, but the grief that happens when you have done every single thing out of alignment with your true self for a really, really long time… it's a different type of grief that truly has the power to destroy you. It's the kind of grief that can trigger a huge meltdown or, you know, turn you into an *angry monster*.

As a master alchemist, now I know that this is the beginning of your Phoenix Spirit coming to the surface. But at the time of being reduced to ashes and bones without a clue as to how I was ever going to recover or if recovery was even possible, I prayed for help and for more guidance, since I had clearly ignored all the clues that were warning me that I'd burn out completely.

People might say I'm hyper-independent and while that is true, they would be reducing me to an archetype that entirely misses the point.

Yes, there was a time when I was hyper-independent, because I felt I could not depend on anyone for help – I didn't even know how to ask for help and maybe there's a part of me that still doesn't, but now I reach out to people and invite them to collaborate on projects, which is my way of saying *"I like you, I trust you and I'd love to create something with you."*

Yes, I continue to be hyper-independent, but my journey of self-growth means I can't stay for too long in the same place or *"level"* unless I'm willing to compromise or give up on my mission – and I am not. As I mentioned earlier, I did it once and it nearly destroyed me.

The pain of losing people is far more bearable than the pain of losing yourself and that's a lesson worth learning at an early age if you're ready to dedicate your life to helping others and humanity.

We must burn down in order to let go of that which is no longer serving us and some of us are stubborn, even when we catch fire and see our whole life go up in flames.

"Let me have one more day here, please."

At one point I was negotiating with the Universe to let me stay at my fifth role a little bit longer, when they had already revealed to me that my purpose on Earth is much bigger than my individual desires and that I had to let go without further discussion.

I know, it's wild – that's my whole life. I've been casually chatting with the Universe as if we're best friends and pretending like everyone else does it, too. But most people are not really tapped into their inner guidance and even when they are, they don't have access to the Divine the way that I do. Some call me crazy, others doubt this connection, and there's a third group that doesn't like me because of it: they want to be among the *"chosen ones"* that hear the Divine, but at the end of the day they don't actually want to do the inner work or hold the responsibilities that come with it – they just want to feel special.

Being chosen by the Universe is not for the weak ones. You are tested, you are judged, you are mishandled, you are redirected, you are used as the bait for people to reveal their true character, you are a pawn in the hands of the Divine as they are proclaiming you to be one of their Masters on Earth.

You feel like you have power and you do, we all do, but that power is not for you and it's not yours to give to others. Your power has everything to do with your calling. Now do you understand why it's so crucial on your journey for you to remain loyal to your purpose and your calling?

The only way people can defeat you is to distract you and get you to give up on your calling using your own free will.

And I've had plenty of people who came into my life with the sole mission of doing just that while operating under the false pretences of wanting to be my friend.

Maybe I've burned some bridges that connected me to genuine hearts, but now I know with certainty that the bridge to my calling and to myself is as strong as ever, which means my job on Earth has already been accomplished.

Yes, anger is a powerful force and you can use it as an ingredient to your alchemy to manifest more of your potential onto Earth. But if anger feels foreign to you, the way that it does to me, there are other emotional states that you can work with to create the life of your dreams – the life of your Higher Self.

When anger shows up on your path, however, consider it an important teacher and don't try to run away from it. Let it show you where your Inner Child requires more of your attention and needs some of the unconditional love only you can give.

Express **YOUR ANGER**

Anger comes and goes in waves just like grief. Let's explore the themes of your life where anger has tried to show you that your boundaries could be stronger and healthier.

Complete the following sentences to clear the way for healing emotions to replace the heavy ones:

ANGER FOR LOSING YOUR WAY
(e.g. routine, habits, hobbies, mindset, attitude)

"I will never allow people to... / people in my life who..."

ANGER FOR LOSING YOUR PEOPLE
(e.g. parents, friends, colleagues, life partner, neighbours)

"I wish I could have said this to... when they..."

ANGER FOR LOSING YOURSELF
(e.g. ideas, purpose, spark, inner Light)

"I will never allow myself to (become)..."

Alchemise **YOUR ANGER**

Anger lowers our frequency and reduces us to a version of ourselves that resembles a shadow. Break through the darkness of anger and channel more of your Inner Light by rewriting the narrative that might be limiting some of your potential right now.

Let's use ANGER to create something useful with it and fill the blank canvas of your next chapter with excitement instead!

Pick one: **LOSING YOUR WAY** | **PEOPLE** | **YOURSELF**

What made you give away your power to others?
Tip: Consider examples where you weren't authentic on purpose
How would you act if you weren't scared of your power?
Challenge: Write an alchemy statement to turn fear into passion

As one of the core emotions, ANGER is a great guide on our Hero's journey. Don't try to ignore it or suppress it – let it show you how to reclaim and channel more of your inner power.

Now it's time to examine FEAR and overcome it!

"Woah... You've changed!"

"The question is – will you?
If the caterpillar never changed,
she would have never figured
out she had wings to fly.
I got my wings!"

Part 3

TO RECLAIM YOURSELF

The

FEAR

A lot can be said about fear since it's proven to be a great ruling force for humanity.

We have been conditioned to OBEY THE RULES with fear for many generations and across many aspects of society, from home life and family traditions to career structures and political systems.

"Do this unless you want X to happen"

"Do this if you love me"

"Do this if you love your neighbours"

Fear enables the manipulation of humans to a whole another level, which would explain the rise of narcissism worldwide.

We have created the perfect conditions to imprison one another in soulless connections that have been so normalised that healthy relationships actually scare us. Our nervous system is on fire, which means that *the act of letting the flow of love in* threatens to put out the fire and since fire has become the norm, the idea of losing it terrifies us.

The absence of adrenaline in connections terrifies us too: *"This just can't be normal: I don't feel on edge 24/7, you don't keep me guessing if you love me or not – if I matter or not. Everything feels safe and predictable... What's the catch?! Deep down you're pretending like all of us, aren't you? Yes, that must be it!"*

We then sabotage ourselves and each other, including the people around us who actually have good intentions for us and love us unconditionally.

Fear has done a lot of damage in society and it has impacted each of us personally from the day of our birth until the day we figure out the power of love, the ultimate antidote to fear.

I was raised with fear more so than with love. For the longest time I thought that the problem was rooted in my own family, but eventually I realised that the whole world has been affected by it.

My parents were raised by parents who were conditioned to fear the system and operate from a state of fear. Their parents were taught to fear in the same way. Our generational trauma goes a long way back to a shared collective past defined by fear – yet against all odds Love has made its way into our life and hearts.

Love is how we ascend above the level of fear. Love is the answer to many of life's problems if we're serious about finding a universal cure to the ongoing conflicts on Earth.

How did fear affect me? In three distinctive ways that shaped much of my identity until I discovered the Love within.

The Fear of **FAILURE**

My fear of failure came down to not being loved when I failed.

If I made a mistake, I would suffer a punishment – from passive aggressive remarks to a full-blown silent treatment that could go on for days.

"I thought you knew better."

If I didn't get a good grade, I would be shouted at.

"How dare you fail me… I mean, yourself."

If I fell and ruined my clothes, I would then be bruised verbally, mentally and emotionally by those who would then have to clean up after my mess as a consequence of my own actions.

"Good girls don't run. Stop embarrassing me and yourself."

When kids fall, they expect their guardians to rush towards them and give them a hug. I often received scolding or warnings – or maybe it wasn't that often, but the times that it did happen scarred me for life.

"I must be perfect or I will not receive love."

No child should live with that thought as part of their innermost belief system.

Imagine having to go through life with so much pressure on your tiny shoulders that you must always be perfect in the eyes of others *(especially those that you trust and love the most)* in order for you to be worthy of receiving their love, help or support…

Well, I don't have to imagine it. I went through it – and I would have continued to go through it until my final breath, but instead I chose to be brave and break the family curse of falling victim to the fear-based programming.

So I allowed myself to make mistakes and then cheered myself in the moments when I ventured out of my comfort zone, knowing that no one had the power to discourage *"my baby steps into the world"* with their judgement or criticism: I had become the change maker, the cycle breaker, the wayshower.

I was transforming into the one who would pave a new way for the generations to come, in ways that my family couldn't imagine or support just yet. They had played a part in breaking other family curses and I was grateful for the opportunities they gave me because of their courage and love, but my purpose required of me to take steps that were even bolder than theirs in order to bring bigger shifts to the status quo of our community and humanity as a whole.

Once more, I had a lot of pressure on my tiny shoulders, but this time I was not afraid to fail, which meant I was nearly ready for success!

The Fear of **SUCCESS**

My favourite book is *Paulo Coelho's* **The Alchemist**, a book treasured by many Souls across the globe – a book that's awakened and inspired many dormant dreamers.

I first discovered it in the library of my high school. It was a small library but there was always something new to discover. Isn't it amazing how every library holds secrets and magic in unmeasurable quantities for those who are willing to seek for answers and keys to help them uncover more of the mysteries of the Universe!

This book offered more than one key that would open multiple doors on my quest for accomplishing my dreams.

Once the loan period expired, I decided not to renew it and returned the library copy of **The Alchemist** back to its shelf. Afterwards, I went straight to the bookstore to buy my own copy.

Since then I've used it as my source of inspiration and wisdom in times of doubt and referred to it when I had to make a big decision in life.

I wrote about it in my university application. I got in!

I brought it with me on numerous flights as I travelled back and forth between my birthplace in Bulgaria and my adopted home in the United Kingdom. I always made it to the other side safely!

I used it as the pivotal force in my career as I realised I had been training to become an Alchemist in my own life as well, along with millions of others who are on the same trajectory globally.

There are many lessons embedded into the storyline, especially when it comes to the fear of failure or pursuing your dreams. It actually took me nearly a decade to be ready to discover a lesson I'd so easily missed... the fear or success.

The fear of success is a powerful gravitational force that will block us from truly allowing our heart to channel the love necessary to attract our dreams.

When we are ready to expand, the Universe will take us on a journey. Sometimes we will be brought into the lives of others or removed from their everyday routine overnight. Other times we will be re-introduced to familiar faces or new Souls will arrive just in time to teach us and show us the way to channelling more of our potential.

The Universe kept whispering to me, *"Dream bigger, you are worthy of so much more than you are envisioning – dream on, child of the Most High!"*

Yot ovory timc I allowed myself to dream, nothing happened. I was still the same, the room around me was still the same, neither the money had arrived, nor the lifestyle that would allow me to reach more people. The list of *"evidence"* against my delusional dreaming only ever expanded as I tried to defend my position of remaining in the comfort zone – or perhaps that was my Ego?

What's worse, the Universe kept removing connections, projects and access to places that were no longer in alignment with who I was and who I was preparing to become.

Instead of obtaining more, every year I had less than the year before. Until there was no one and nothing left from my old life.

And so I had no more excuses to hold onto.

Once I had the space to dream as big as I wanted to and actually do something about it, all I had to do was overcome my fear of being seen in my authenticity, and soon enough I realised that the fear of losing myself once again was much stronger.

So I started taking steps in the direction of my wildest dreams and I allowed myself to *"receive"* or *"ground"* the dreams directly from my Higher Self opposed to trying to figure them out as the version of myself that had been walking on planet Earth for a little over three decades.

That's when the magic started pouring from me and I had no other choice but to believe in myself and overcome my fear of being seen as my true self because this was the golden ticket to the life of my dreams.

I was the golden ticket. I was the golden child. I was the one made of gold, perfectly designed by the Divine for a time like this one and no amount of fear would be able to stop the portal of love and creativity that had been unlocked within me.

So I continued to walk on my journey to self-actualisation with one clear mission in mind: to reach as many Souls as possible and unlock their potential too.

The Fear of **BEING YOURSELF**

It doesn't really matter how much inner work you do and how supportive your environment becomes, there will still be days when you have to face doubt and anxiety when it comes to being yourself.

Give yourself permission to sit in the uncomfortableness, as you make more room to hold all parts of your Inner Child that may have been previously rejected by those who were supposed to love you in all of your colours and seasons.

When so much of our early onboarding on Earth has taught us to pretend to be someone else in order to receive love, our wiring for belonging will occasionally trick us into believing that *we might lose the people we love the most* if we don't curate our behaviour to match their exact requirements.

But we're not machines or pieces of software that need coding to meet the exact requirements of the project developer. If anything, we are the most advanced form of AI, which allows us to reinvent ourselves in real time based on what serves us and what's blocking our personal evolution on Earth.

We are living, breathing humans with extraordinary abilities to create, innovate and expand when we allow ourselves to dream.

The people who *truly* love you are those who have recognised your Soul and you can never lose them because they are not attached to expectations of who you should be or how you should act, since they have already witnessed the greatness of your Spirit and know their life is richer, more meaningful with your presence in it.

Being yourself is a win-win choice.

Sure, you will absolutely lose some connections, because they were never aligned with your Soul's evolutionary path – a path that had been pre-planned and designed for you long before you arrived into your human vessel that represents who you are in the 3D world today.

But more importantly, you will absolutely attract Souls who are on the same expansive journey as you – your soul family who will support you unconditionally and cheer you on as you unlock more of your potential and hidden gifts.

The fear of being yourself comes down to the fear of being alone: abandoned, rejected, ignored, ridiculed, punished, forgotten.

No one actually fears being themselves, what we all fear is losing the love that comes from belonging in the world. When we've been rejected for who we are, we learn to *"lock"* our authenticity away, so that people don't deny us the love that's otherwise given to us freely.

But there's a source of Love that comes from within all of us that cannot be stopped, unless we block it and even then it will find a way to flow.

We are the source of Love we so desperately seek to find out in the world, so how can we ever lose it if we don't stop ourselves from loving in the first place?

So as naive as it may appear, the antidote to your fear of being yourself is to love yourself unconditionally. It's as simple as that!

Since the world is a mirror that reveals to you all of your greatest fears and dreams as well as your biggest lessons and mistakes, it also reflects back to you the kind of love that you give.

Forgive the people who couldn't love you. Forgive the people who betrayed you. Forgive the people who hurt you. Their main job was to trick and test you: *"Are you going to stop believing in love now?"*

Yet here you are, still full of love and hope for tomorrow's world.

You have passed the ultimate test – the test of love. Not many get to say they've passed the test of love with flying colours and graduate to become a true Divine Messenger on Earth that will be added to the Hall of Fame in the Spiritual realm.

Congratulations!

You're ready to explore the path of COURAGE. What, did you think that your quest for more meaning would come to an end once you overcame your biggest fears? The real exciting part of your life is actually about to begin!

Feel **YOUR FEAR**

Fear paralyses us. It tricks us into believing in stories that aren't real. But the opposite of fear can help us escape those stories: love, imagination, passion! Let's activate your creative side.

Complete the following sentences to give your FEAR enough room to grow, so that you can realise it's not real – it's an illusion:

FEAR OF FAILURE
(e.g. career, school, relationships, community judgement)

"What would people think if I didn't / couldn't…"

FEAR OF SUCCESS
(e.g. lifestyle changes, relationship status, community exposure)

"How would my life change if I actually did X, Y or Z?"

FEAR OF BEING YOURSELF
(e.g. judgement, acceptance, criticism)

"What would my mother / father say if they knew I was…"

Forgive **YOUR FEAR**

Whether we like to admit it or not, a lot of our personal fear comes from the beliefs we acquired when we were children. Deeply rooted in our subconscious mind, you'll find all the reasons for your behaviour today – time to take a deep dive into examining your belief system together. Let's use FEAR as the starting point of what you really desire and slowly find the COURAGE to alchemise it into action!

Pick one: **FAILURE | SUCCESS | BEING YOURSELF**

What did you learn from your biggest failure in life?
Tip: Consider failures from different age periods in your growth
What's a dream for your life that actually scares you?
Challenge: Write an acceptance speech for your Dream Award!

Fear exists on a spectrum just like all the other emotions, but we often fail to understand whether the anxiousness we're feeling is the expression of doubt or excitement. Fear shows up to prepare us ahead of big changes, either way.

Next on our list is COURAGE – the biggest antidote to Fear!

"How are you so fearless?"

"It's alchemy. Surrender a thing to receive another. You see, fear doesn't get along with love: one has to go in order for the other to thrive. I traded fear for Love!"

The
COURAGE

Have you ever been told you're courageous in your life in times when you followed your heart, trusted your intuition or acted in alignment with what's right?

Being the bigger person in situations requires a certain level of courage, because there's always a possibility that you're wrong.

Courage doesn't always mean that you have full clarity, confidence or understanding about a situation, but that you trust the endgame will work out in your favour.

To lead with courage is to trust the unknown as much as you trust yourself.

The Courage to **TRY AGAIN**

The word failure doesn't really exist in my vocabulary. To me, failure is about staying the same for a really long time and I've fully embraced self-growth as my lifestyle. In other words, I've embraced change as the norm.

To fail is to not try at all. The courage to try again is essentially the courage to fail – time and time and time again.

I am known to be a risk taker among friends, family members and my wider network. Even if the risks are calculated, they are still risks and that makes them so tricky to pursue, which is why so many people have told me I'm brave over the years.

"Oh, you're so brave to live abroad!"

"Oh, you're so brave to go alone!"

"Oh, you're so brave to not care about what people think!"

"Oh, you're so brave to follow your dreams!"

Sure, some compliments have been backhanded, others sincere, but the fact remains – I am indeed brave to remain loyal to my authenticity in a world that encourages us all to get lost in the trivial routines and give up on our true purpose.

The courage to try again is not something triumphant, or rather, it shouldn't be. We should all be encouraged to try again as part of our self-growth exploration.

Life is a series of experiments to those who have unlocked more of their potential, because they understand that the only way to learn something new is to try something new, whether you perceive it as a risk or as an investment.

Chimamanda Ngozi Adichie once wrote that we should all be feminists, but I'd argue that before that can happen – we should all become risk takers who know the value of trusting oneself.

The courage to try again is not a privilege, it's a necessity. We must all remember the power of our tongue, thoughts, intentions and actions and use that power to *try again* with more conviction of the results we're trying to achieve.

Some people might be born to be leaders, teachers or artists, but the world by design is not divided into winners and losers.

The only way to win is to continue to play (in) the Game of Life. How you win is entirely dependent on you. While some people cheat and steal in order to get to the top, others lead with love, kindness and collaboration.

There isn't a single definition of the word *"success"*, so you must decide what's yours, but there's certainly almost no way to win if you don't even attempt to try again after defeat.

Don't let your whole life be defined by a single defeat or a series of failures, because the power of your Higher Self is greater than words could ever describe it.

The courage to try again is to summon your Spirit and shift your perspective from a short-term strategy of surviving to a long-term strategy of building an abundant life for yourself and the people you love.

The Courage to **ASK FOR MORE**

It's time to introduce more lessons from the mentors that appeared on my path when I needed guidance: these are mindset shortcuts that helped me shift the trajectory of my life for the better, precisely because they guided me towards accessing higher levels of courage.

A sentence I'll never forget is this one:

"They need you more than you need them."

I was at the start of my career journey and I had to make a choice – to stay at a role that didn't make me happy and keep my paycheck (which affected both my performance and my overall well-being negatively), or be honest with my employees and risk losing my job altogether.

My indirect mentor reminded me that I was a talented person with a lot of potential and much to give to the world, regardless of the company I worked for. Even as a junior employee, I was a stellar employee and that is priceless in any economy.

When you show up for others with great optimism for the work that you do, your employer really needs you more than you need them – talented high performers have the power to level up entire brands, which is why few companies can retain *passionate* talented people in their team for long periods of time: their talent is destined for great heights and not all business enterprises make it to the top.

I chose to be courageous and decided to go for a lower paying position that was fully aligned with my skills, passion and purpose, which then allowed me to find the next job role as I had maintained my life path to authentic self-actualisation.

It was years before I referred to this advice once more:

"They need you more than you need them."

This time I was in a role that perfectly fit me and offered me great creative growth as well as opportunities to develop additional skills. The problem? I wasn't getting forward with my career – nothing I ever did was enough for me to be recognised fully for everything that I brought into *and with* my performance.

Once again, I had to be honest with myself.

Money was never the key driver when making pivotal decisions in my life, such as choosing a degree or a career path and even my clothes as long as they accurately reflected my authenticity.

While my role at the time fit my authenticity, it didn't match my self-worth, which was increasing every day that I challenged myself to be more honest.

This time I spoke words I'll never forget and they kinda echoed across all realms as this was a statement from my Soul to all living beings that I had ever encountered during my existence:

"You've benefited from me not knowing my worth. I love my job, but I need more and I'm not talking about recognition – the time for that is long gone."

This is a statement that you're allowed to say at work. A statement that would otherwise suggest the end of a romantic relationship.

We enter professional contracts to exchange our skills and time for money, whereas we form friendships and partnerships in order to share our time together and build side by side.

Yes, companies offer us the *"family package"* as part of the employee branding, but you're ultimately paid for your time and dedication, and as I said above, I'm a stellar employee – it's in my name.

The more I pursued authenticity, the more my life expanded in ways that I didn't even fully understand what to make of at the time. It felt like I was becoming who I always wanted to be while parts of me were disintegrating

One at a time, outdated versions of me started getting erased from my daily behaviour: the people-pleaser, the perfectionist, the one who was scared to ask for what she really wanted, the person who didn't know how to say **"No"**.

Yes, that was a big blindspot for me. One of my mentors caught me off guard when he said this to me:

"Do you know that I've never heard you say "No" to people when they come to you for help? Not once. I mean, who does that?!"

My initial response was, *"I never want people to feel like they don't have anyone to help them, because that's how I've spent my life."*

But then I thought some more about it and realised that I wasn't really helping them or serving the world as generously as I could. In fact, this was a false statement within my own belief system that was guiding my behaviour in a way that wasn't healthy towards me.

Saying *"No"* is not impolite. It's an expression of honesty when you lack the capacity to support someone.

Yes, you can always make time and space to embrace other people's problems and pain and help them overcome their hurdles. I spent 30 years of my life doing just that, only to realise that I wasn't really being of service – I was trying to prove myself *"worthy"* to others all the while ignoring my own aching heart through offering my love to everyone but me.

The day I finally said **"No"** to the rest of the world was the day I said **"Yes"** to my own healing journey and returning back to my purpose.

Until that day happened, however, I had attracted a lot of people who relied on me for my listening and problem-solving skills: people who looked to me for inspiration and authenticity they could *"borrow"* from without ever intending to return what they had essentially stolen to supply their own identity, which had become another blindspot for me that another mentor dear to me pointed out in a random conversation at a random bar on a random Thursday night.

"Stella, it kinda sounds like you've got the wrong people around you if you cannot celebrate life, or you know, what matters to you with them!"

The courage to ask for more comes with an avalanche of losses, goodbyes and destruction. But that avalanche also makes way for new opportunities and connections to arrive.

When you're finally ready to ask for more, you have to be prepared to let go of everything that is no longer in alignment with you, which is usually the entire foundation of your previous life.

To let go of all that you know is to experience the grief of shedding your old life without anyone to hold your hand or offer you an arm to cry on. It's a journey you must take on your own, because you've finally learned the value of your innermost Self – who you are at your core.

It feels like I had to abandon a whole version of myself overnight, but the metamorphosis didn't happen in a single day. It happened over the course of many sleepless nights, early mornings, afternoons packed with hard work, evenings where no one saw my tears and breakfast dates with my laptop as I was seeking to channel my potential and get back on track with my own goals.

Eventually, I realised that I wasn't doing the journey alone. For one, I had my Spirit Team watching over me, but also – I had successfully reconnected with my Inner Child and my Higher Self.

The Courage to **DO IT YOUR WAY**

There's nothing more courageous than defending your authenticity at all costs.

The courage to be yourself is the courage to:

- Fail
- Try again
- Do it your way

- Trust the process
- Go alone
- Ask for more
- Say NO
- Break free from the norms
- Escape the comfort zone
- Question society
- Propose innovative solutions
- Channel your potential
- Forgive and release
- Speak up
- Share your feelings
- Leave unhealthy environments
- Enter new rooms
- Explore possibilities
- Ascend above your circumstances
- Sit in the silence with a smile on your face
- Change your routine
- Believe in your dreams
- Call out abuse
- Protect your heart
- Honour peace
- Befriend yourself

We build our courage through action. The more we challenge ourselves and accept opportunities for growth, the braver we become.

I've done many things alone, not by choice but out of necessity. If I didn't have the courage to go through multiple seasons of life on my own, I wouldn't have become the person I am today.

If I didn't preserve my passion for music, my creative ideas, my interest in books and movies, my wiring for philosophy and psychology, my inner drive to channel more of my potential and ask big questions, *to name a few examples*, I would have lost a huge part of my true identity. But in order for me to preserve all aspects of my authenticity, I had to persevere on my own. Why?

No one around me cared about life the way I did and this meant I had two choices: to ignore everything that made me who I was in order to participate in relationships with others or leave people who were not aligned with my true self behind.

For the longest time, I attempted to do both.

I continued to pour into my growth in private as I downsized my interests, goals and achievements in public. Not once did I give up on my authentic self, but I stopped sharing it and that *stole from my destiny* in the same way people tried to steal ideas and energy from me.

I listened to everyone else's essence and gave them space to grow in my company since I could see the potential that was dormant within them, just waiting for someone to believe in them – gladly taking the role of being a messenger of hope and support. An endless supply of optimism and cheerleader energy!

Deep down I was hoping that one day they'd see life through my perspective and join me on my quest for excellence, growth and positive change, but somehow they never did.

In hindsight, there were people – friends, colleagues and roommates – who realised who I was and what my true mission on Earth was, but they thought of my pursuit of changing the world through self-growth as too much work to actually do it themselves.

They never said it in plain words, but their actions showed me time and time again that my presence didn't really matter so long as they had access to my energy, since I was the one who could hold their problems and heal them too without a single complaint.

Call them energetic parasites or insecure peers, they blocked me from ascending to the person I was always meant to become, because I allowed them to – I stayed in connections where my presence was not celebrated, but tolerated.

Yet those who celebrated me turned out to be even worse: at least those who had a tolerance for my authenticity were honest enough to show their true feelings.

There's grief that comes when you figure out that the people you considered friends were merely people who benefited from your energy, but it gets worse.

The disgust arrives when you finally understand that some of the people you've allowed closest to your heart are the ones who'd have ripped it apart in seconds if they could, because your destruction would translate into their victory of fully stealing and wearing your essence. I can still see their hands reaching out to my heart – their Souls lost in the shadow of their shame.

These were people who were so captivated by me that they thought they could befriend me to steal my essence – one feature and skill at a time – and dump their flaws onto me through erasing my values with the words they chose to speak about me to their own community when I was not around.

The courage to rise above betrayals and narcissism is by far one of the greatest achievements I can add to my name, even if the only witnesses to my silent battles with jealous friends and insecure foes are my Spirit Guides.

There's no courage in revenge, only cowardice and fear.

I am still finding words to express my shock from the realisation that not all friends come into your life to support, uplift and love you unconditionally. Some come just to extract information and sabotage your plans. And the only way to figure out what role every person would play in your life is to let them show you who they are without expectations or regulations – that's the trust fall.

Do you dare to trust the world? It starts with having the courage to trust yourself.

Once you've been hurt by someone you loved, the next betrayal doesn't affect you as much. Loving people is a risk you must take in order to experience what it means to be human. But first, you must be courageous enough to fall in love with yourself!

The courage to *do life your way* is the courage to pick yourself time and time again until you align with people, places and opportunities that can meet you exactly where you are: physically, mentally, emotionally and spiritually.

There's courage in saying *"I'll try again"* as well as in your sincere determination to change your approach.

It takes about the same amount of courage to pursue your dreams as it does to admit that you're wrong.

We all change constantly. To have the courage to embrace your metamorphosis and embrace the natural flow of changes is to allow for the next phase of your evolution to be completed.

What's on the other side? The next version of you!

Channel **YOUR COURAGE**

Courage is inherent to all of us, but some use it on a daily basis whereas others rely on it in a time of need. No matter what group you belong to, it's essential that you recognise the power of your Spirit and the miracles you're capable of co-creating!

Complete the following sentences to remind yourself of the greatness of your Spirit and how far you've come on your journey:

COURAGE TO TRY AGAIN
(e.g. family, love, work, entrepreneurship, friendships, hobbies)

"The area of my life I have failed and tried again the most is…"

COURAGE TO ASK FOR MORE
(e.g. career, living situation, partner, romance, adventures)

"I will never forget the day I had the courage to demand more…"

COURAGE TO DO IT YOUR OWN WAY
(e.g. personal goals, professional ambitions, societal changes)

"I'm the first in my family to…"

Share **YOUR COURAGE**

Failure and success are interconnected in the same way fear and courage are interlinked. There's a duality to everything in life: let's integrate more of your life experiences and the lessons attached to them to restore your inner balance.

Let's figure out how you can share your courage with others and inspire them to believe in themselves the way that you do!

Pick one: **TRY AGAIN | ASK FOR MORE | DO IT YOUR WAY**

What are you afraid of losing if you dream bigger?
Tip: Consider what you will "lose" if you succeed
What makes you courageous? List some examples!
Challenge: Ask 5 people you trust if they view you as courageous

Courage can be found within us at all times. Remember that your inherent wisdom has already equipped you with everything you need to accomplish your wildest dreams and bring positive change on Earth by being yourself.

Don't let the MIND tell you otherwise – let's have a look into it!

"Who taught you
how to be so brave?"

"I learned it myself. When
people laughed at me and
left me to figure things out
on my own, I understood that
courage was always within!"

TO REFINE YOURSELF

The
MIND

Logic will get you from A to Z, but when you activate your creative intelligence and use more of your right brain – you can come up with a solution for anything.

Einstein was trying to tell us that imagination is more than just a skill for artists and young people, it's the key to self-mastery and success in life.

Your ideas are everything!

Your ideas are seeds that you can plant in the garden of your conscious mind and water them to push your legacy into its blooming season through activating the hidden power of your subconscious mind. This is a message that's been delivered from multiple teachers, including Napoleon Hill, Louise Hay, Eckhart Tolle and Rhonda Byrne.

When you combine the abilities of your brain with the potential that's stored in your connection with your Higher Self, a whole new world opens up within and before you: that's how you trigger the release of your kinetic energy to manifest your dream reality, but first you must learn to overcome yourself.

The habit of being yourself is the hardest one to break. What I mean by this is that much of our life is automated by the time we reach age 7. So if we decide to shift our reality at the age of 30, there's a lot to investigate, integrate and improve in order to align with the version of life we want to experience as our norm.

I began shifting my habits at the age of 28. That was the year I got two important books: one helped me a lot, the other's yet to assist me on my journey.

'Atomic Habits' by James Clear helped me understand the framework for shifting your identity, and uprooting all the false mirrors that are distorting one's belief system, through a more conscious and practical way of setting goals.

'The 5AM Club' by Robin Sharma showed me the importance of an early start, so that you can reconnect with your Higher Self and Nature before you venture out into the world and use your energy to co-create with your neighbours.

I am yet to build a routine since my energy goes through massive ups and downs as I'm purging heavy emotions on a subconscious level (as well as on a Soul level) and channelling a lot of ideas from my Higher Self – ideas that were blocked for a number of years in the past decade.

In other words, I've got a lot of catching up to do since my heart's become so clogged from living out of alignment with my true authentic life path that my mind's now operating at full capacity to make up for the lost time of being disconnected from my own inner Divine guidance!

It's safe to say that choosing to return to my true self was the starting point of a long journey that began with self-growth at the level of the mind (*the conscious mind where thoughts are getting processed*) and later on continued at the level of the heart (*the subconscious mind where all complex emotions get stored and plugged into your belief system; also where you will find the source of all of your triggers*).

I couldn't have done my self-growth journey alone, yet I did it without much help. The word *"self"* implies that only you can make the choice to embark on the journey, knowing it's going to be a difficult adventure, but an adventure nonetheless.

I had a mentor who pushed me further into the ocean of my potential, a mentor who tried to block my path ahead as he painted a picture of a false mirage in the open seas and a mentor who asked me the most courageous question of all. This was all at the level of the conscious mind!

At the level of the subconscious mind, things got much darker as images of friends and family members came to the surface – people who were supposed to be on my team who had been supporting everyone else but me for a very long time.

What's shocking isn't that you have to do things on your own, but that it is your only choice if you wish to progress in life and accomplish your purpose.

Using your free will to make independent decisions is not a burden, it's a gift. But the world we live in is highly co-dependent and designed to encourage toxic tendencies every step of the way to cripple us as we postpone our personal evolution.

Many people are blocked from accessing their own Higher Self, just like I was, due to unhealthy habits, unhealthy connections and unhealthy beliefs about themselves.

After many years of restrictions, I broke free from the jail my Inner Child was locked in and this is how you can do it, too.

The Gift of **FREE WILL**

I once went on a rescue mission for the Inner Child of someone I cared about. They had their Inner Child trapped in a huge castle and while all the doors were unlocked, they didn't dare venture outside. They were trapped inside due to the trauma they had experienced of loving without being loved in return: the rejection, the shame, the abandonment, the numbness, the loss, the denial. They were trapped inside of their own subconscious mind with all of these heavy emotions and the deep core belief that no one truly cared about them.

Then I showed up in their life – in their castle – and I let myself in. Once I found them, I gently opened the door of their prison cell (*yes, their imagination had created a very convincing scenario in which they were actually a prisoner who was unable to leave, that's how persuasive and powerful our inner narrative can be when it comes to restricting or liberating us*) and flashed them a golden key.

"Hey, I'm here to bring you out. Let's go!"

That's the thing: the door was already open, but they didn't know it and it would not have made sense to tell them that. They were so much under the spell of the false programming that a part of them might have rejected me if they realised I was an *"intruder"* based on the parameters their consciousness was using to co-create side by side with their Ego.

They were very much disconnected from their Inner Child and their Higher Self, so I had to speak to them in a manner that allowed me to remain an authority figure who is simply transporting a prisoner, but in the meantime I was freeing them from the illusion that they were deeply broken and therefore unlovable.

Again, they couldn't know about it until much further in the process of our time together, because otherwise they would not have listened to me – they would have rejected me the way a broken body might reject a healthy heart during a transplant because it misses its original owner's heart. Some wounds are beyond repair on our own and we need the help of others.

This is when I first met the Dragons. On our way out, we were attacked by a Dragon who was assigned to guard the castle where their Inner Child was trapped. It's unclear whether this was an attack on their identity or an inside mission where they had personally asked their Dragon to watch out for any intruders.

But this was the moment I realised that there was a mighty Dragon beside me, too, as I was escorting my friend out of their man-made torture castle.

Ancient Souls have ancient protectors as we are visiting Earth to advance our evolution, so that can bring positive change into the societal structures through our example.

Remember what I said about our ideas? They are seeds that we get to plant in our garden and then water them with the power of our emotions. So when we begin to flourish, our creations slowly but surely establish the foundation of our legacy. This is the manifesting process of self-actualisation!

Well, this story is a great example of what happens when a person hasn't healed their trauma and reconnected with their Inner Child.

My friend had built an impressive castle upon lands that could fit in and support a whole village, but its impenetrable walls instead served as a structure to imprison themselves. As a result, the garden of their imagination which surrounded the castle for miles ahead in every direction was empty – it was green, fresh, full of fertile soil but no seeds were planted in it.

The owner of the garden was absent: he was reliving the memories of his past and the pain attached to them, or perhaps coming up with scenarios in which new people might enter his heart's space to further inflict pain onto him, because deep down he believed that's all he deserved – pain.

We are all gardeners. Our Ego might trick us into thinking that building a fortress is the best usage of our time: *"Finally we're safe – no one can attack us in here!"*

But who's in the castle with you? Are you ignoring the seeds that you've been given that can birth a new world onto the Earth? Are you hiding from the world, because you're too scared of pain and rejection? Is there a part of you that's scared to be seen for the first time for all of your gifts and talents?

Your most abundant life begins when you are ready to leave the comfort zone of whatever structure your Ego has persuaded you to build as a hiding place.

On the other side of fear, there is an open field where you get to meet the Inner Children of fellow brave Souls who have also made their way to Earth to co-create amazing shifts for people of all ages, and above all, for the future generations.

Ready to meet your Inner Child and discover more of your inner magic? Let your heart love again.

Fall in love with life. Fall in love with Nature. Fall in love with your work. Fall in love with your body. Fall in love with the food you prepare. Fall in love with your morning routine. Fall in love with books, podcasts, research, data, stories, destinations, the Sun, the Moon, the wind on your skin every time you leave home, the fingertips that allow you to experience more of the world around you.

The gift of free will doesn't expire and no one can take it away from you. It's your birthright, so long as you remember it and who you are.

One of the best ways to use your gift of free will is to choose to pursue what excites your heart – that's not only the key to your happiness, but a sure indication that you're moving in alignment with your purpose. But first, let's talk more about your personal evolution!

The Choice of **SELF-GROWTH**

Self-growth is a choice. A conscious choice, to be precise. It's an investment into building a life for yourself that your Future Self will thank you for.

There are short-term and long-term benefits, but the rewards of pursuing personal growth arrive much later on your journey, so you have to be 100% sure you want the best for yourself – and keep in mind that some people are happy with a mediocre life where they get to see other people plant seeds and become skillful, successful gardeners while they make it a habit to pluck out their own hairs and complain about their wasted potential.

Self-growth is a bold choice that automatically makes you an Alchemist Trainee or an Apprentice Alchemist!

You begin to work with your Higher Self more consciously as you openly question everything and experiment with your routine. There are two key elements that you will need to work with when you choose self-growth: Fire and Earth.

Fire connects you further with your Higher Self, your true calling and how you can be of service to others through unlocking more of your authenticity.

Earth helps you master your daily habits as the element that brings more stability to your identity by reaffirming the neural pathways that must stay through action (*e.g. go to the gym and show up for your fitness routine*) and those that have to go away for good through skipping the action (*e.g. turn away from the alcohol aisle in the supermarket and get more fresh food instead*).

Self-growth starts with a choice, therefore it is the Air domain of thinking, ideas and mindset that determines the beginning of a brand new chapter in your life.

It is then through tapping into your unexplored potential that you get to venture into the Fire realm of your Spiritual or Higher Self, the birthplace of your Soul – also known as Source.

Finally, you bring the transformation down to Earth by applying action, which brings all the pieces of your inner transformation together, so that you can show up with an upgraded energy and attract a new reality that matches your vibration.

Self-growth is more than a series of choices. It's real alchemy!

You might be wondering, *"Wait, where's the element of Water?"*

Well, there's a whole chapter dedicated to it, because the healing journey that happens at the level of your heart and your emotions is too complex to fit in a single sentence, but the truth is your baby steps into self-growth don't require much emotion – you just have to keep showing up using the power of your free will as a way to strengthen your new identity and rewire your conscious mind.

The real work with the element of Water begins once you've made some significant changes in your lifestyle to be able to take a proper dive into your subconscious mind.

I had done a little over 1 year of self-growth before my Higher Self guided me onto my healing journey, which lasted about 2 more years of consistent journaling, meditation, visualisation, somatic practices, feeling my emotions, revisiting memories and integrating energy as part of reclaiming my inner power until I was feeling like *"myself"* once more.

This book is the product of my healing journey as much as it is part of my mission to help people reconnect with their true authenticity and purpose during their lifetime, so that they can live with more meaning and create positive change for the next generations.

The Ability to **THINK FOR YOURSELF**

Every self-help book is designed to remind you of knowledge that's already within you: knowledge that you can access at any point in your life by reconnecting with your Higher Self. That's the tricky part!

If you haven't established a connection with your Higher Self, it's very likely that you are also disconnected from your Inner Child.

It might sound trivial or too simple to be true, but there's no better way to reconnect with your true self than to do your own research:

- Read books
- Explore articles
- Listen to podcasts
- Follow creators
- Watch different media outlets
- Learn different ideologies
- Form your opinions – then change them

As part of your mind work and working with the element of Air, it's essential that you begin to build your own philosophy for life, which borrows inspiration and ideas from people you admire for their work and contribution to society.

Collect as much information, different points of view and data sources as you can. Then think about it and analyse what you find useful, interesting, boring, disturbing, exciting and even familiar. The ability to think for yourself will get you to new horizons, new heights and new possibilities that far surpass the capabilities of even the most advanced computer.

In the process of consciously learning about the world around and within you, you will begin to "unlock" memories and inner knowledge that's always been part of your consciousness: all of it blocked by the firewall that we experience when we arrive on Earth until we are ready to wake up from the programming and ascend to the level necessary for *our real work* to begin.

Your ability to think for yourself is not just helpful when the time comes to vote for a new political representative in your community or to get your degree from university. It's the prerequisite to *"downloading"* your authenticity blueprint, which can arrive in pieces or as a whole avalanche of data that drops into your consciousness overnight as you awaken into a completely different timeline than the one you went to bed from.

The Universe loves to support people who are on a quest of self-actualisation and the choice to invest in your self-growth will get you on top of the promotion list that accelerates change makers who are ready to lead and fulfil their wildest dreams.

Develop the ability to think for yourself and you will be given the opportunity to help other people begin to plant seeds into their own gardens. That's the real power of self-growth: you invest into yourself, so that you can pour from the abundant mindset of your garden onto the fertile soil of future gardeners.

Ask the Universe to help you get unstuck and you'll experience the most profound delivery of ideas. What you do with those ideas will determine your future, so treat your seeds with great care and appreciation for they are your gold on Earth!

Explore **YOUR MIND**

The conscious mind is far less complicated than the subconscious mind, but it's still a challenge to rewire your thought patterns. Let's start small and work our way to the big positive affirmations.

Complete the following sentences to upgrade your inner wiring:

THE GIFT OF FREE WILL
(e.g. family, love, work, entrepreneurship, friendships, hobbies)

"I will never stop doing … even if I have to do it alone."

THE CHOICE OF SELF-GROWTH
(e.g. career, living situation, partner, romance, adventures)

"I take great pleasure in learning about…"

THE ABILITY TO THINK FOR YOURSELF
(e.g. personal goals, professional ambitions, societal changes)

"One of my favourite controversial opinions is…"

Expand **YOUR MIND**

Expanding your mind begins with giving yourself permission to embody more of your authentic self. Stop apologising for who you are and instead boldly represent your true identity with every thought, action and emotion that supports your movement in life. Let's expand your MIND to new heights by introducing you to new perspectives!

Pick one: **FREE WILL | SELF-GROWTH | THINK FOR YOURSELF**

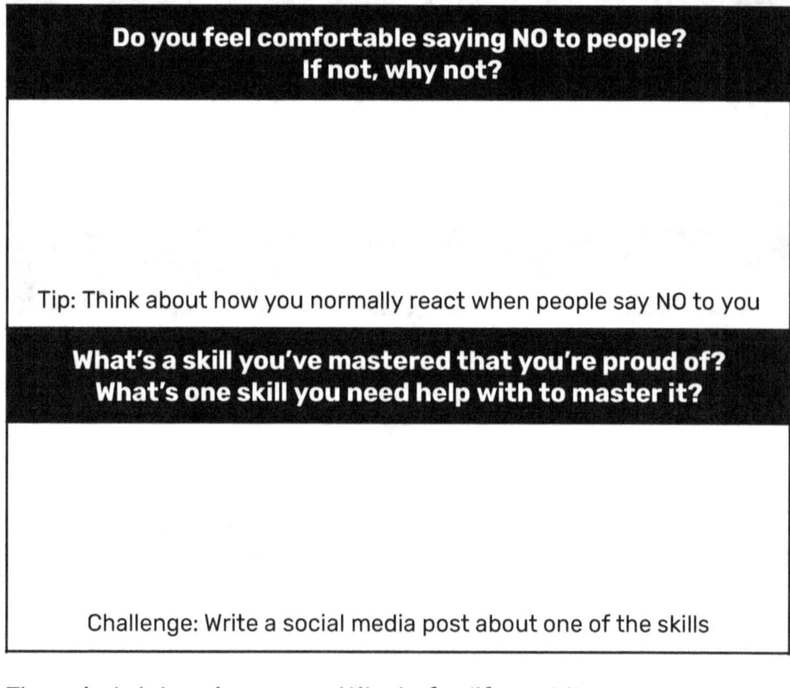

The mind determines our attitude for life and it can empower us to great heights or disempower us from dreaming altogether. Keep expanding your MIND to channel more of your potential.

Can you guess our next stop? It's the HEART, of course!

"Why are you so optimistic?"

"It's simple. I understand the Laws of the Universe. Positivity is not just a state of mind, it's a force field that can move the unmovable. You can say that I'm a Change Agent and I'm not the only one!"

The
HEART

I think I channelled my first love letter when I was 23. It came right from my Soul and spoke of love that could be felt at a Soul level. It wasn't bound or defined by the physical space and it didn't seek the physical aspects of a relationship. It was simply a declaration of Love that wanted to be expressed: from one Soul to another.

When I was 27, I received a channelled love letter from someone else who had thought it essential that they express the emotions bubbling up in their heart as a way of being more in alignment with their Soul's Truth.

Well, let me ask you this:

"When's the last time you expressed your love to yourself?"

We are so eager to give our heart to other people in our pursuit to be noticed, to be of service, to help and uplift others, to show our commitment and loyalty.

But who's the person that's with you 24/7, whether you like it or not? You.

Aren't you worthy of being noticed, supported and loved all throughout your life?

There's no substitute for the love you have for yourself, even if society will have you believe that self-love is selfish. Once your inner cup of love is full, you can then

go out and share it freely with others – without expectations, judgement or resentment.

But there's a strange phenomenon you might notice when you begin to look for ways to apply more self-love in your life: you won't know how!

We have been taught how to recognise love, how to practise it and how to give it to other people in multiple ways as part of our social onboarding into the world.

Yet no one really ever teaches you how to love yourself, so that you can get to the heart of who you are and maintain your sense of Self as you continue your personal evolution on Earth.

No wonder so many of us get lost in life: we don't even know who we are to begin with. Then there's the matter of being unable to recognise our own needs, to apply the proper self-care and to protect our authenticity at all times.

Authenticity is the way of self-actualisation, but very few Souls know what it means to be authentic, because fitting in has been the norm for so long. To stand out and show a different side of yourself and humanity is considered eccentric, weird and even a little bit wrong.

Our hearts are aching. Can you feel it – the collective pain that's in the air? Pain that your parents have felt and their parents, too. Pain that your friends are feeling and their family, too. Pain that is in the hearts of your colleagues and your boss, too.

This pain of inauthenticity has had our hearts captured in a trap for a long time, waiting for someone to feel it, understand it and integrate it like a skillful Alchemist who knows the value of every single ingredient.

Yes, pain is part of being alive. In fact, pain demands your attention in the same way that joy seeks opportunities to spend time with you. Only Pain would never admit to such a thing – that she needs you to notice her and befriend her, unlike her equal partner Joy who is always excited to see you and spend more time with you, just like in the Pixar animation *'Inside Out'*.

This is the moment you become an Alchemist and re-introduce yourself to your own mind, body, heart and soul. The choice to feel your pain is not only an invitation to meet more aspects of your true authentic self, but an opportunity to build a stronger relationship with your Inner Child – the one who's been carrying all the heavy emotions, anticipating your return back home to yourself.

Ready to make that choice? Let's do it together.

The Choice to **FEEL YOUR EMOTIONS**

You might have heard a quote that goes along the lines of *"Pain travels through a family line until someone is brave enough to feel it"*.

Sometimes the pain you're feeling isn't yours.

Sometimes you can tap into the pain of your mother or father, your siblings or grandparents, the neighbour or a colleague, a friend who's based miles away from you or even your pet.

When you begin to feel your emotions, you will activate more of your intuition, which in turn will unlock any intuitive gifts you possess – they are often referred to as spiritual or psychic gifts. Simply put, this is you working with more of the right side of the brain where the magic of your emotional intelligence happens!

The ability to relate to other people's emotions is, of course, known as empathy.

But to be able to actually feel and grasp the depths of the emotional state of someone else is an aspect of clairsentience, which can be considered the mother of empathy.

The choice to feel your emotions has a ripple effect. It starts with you, but once you've done the energetic clearing needed to reconnect with your Inner Child, work your way through pain and remove the limiting beliefs that have been blocking you from living authentically, your sense of belonging in the world will transform as well.

The Ability of **SELF-HEALING**

Did you know that there are memories that we ignore, because there's too much pain associated with them and it's precisely this pain that holds us back in life?

I started my self-healing journey with a single childhood memory. It was nothing important, yet my Inner Child had turned it into a core belief, so I knew I had to face it and heal it.

The first time I *"travelled back to it"* in my memory, I just felt the pain amidst the fog, because a part of me didn't want to remember.

The second time, I was able to visualise myself as that little girl who was walking back from school who had her grandma's hand holding her firmly. There was almost joy in that memory – if one didn't investigate beyond the surface!

The third time, I could recall more aspects of the scene that started to explain the association with pain. My tights were ruined and there was blood on my knee, I had fallen earlier as I was chasing a friend. Normal childhood experience, right?

The fourth time, I realised that the pain wasn't really about my knee. I noticed I was nervous to look at my grandma's face. When I finally turned towards her, there was animosity.

The fifth time, I was brave enough to explore her reaction further and why I was reacting so strongly to that memory.

What was stored in this one seemingly insignificant memory was a pattern for the relationship I had experienced between myself and my first primary guardian in life. It's only natural that this relationship had defined my belief system around all relationships – a child trusts her guardians for guidance unconditionally.

What my Inner Child was thinking at the time of the memory was *"Maybe I deserve the animosity, because I did not follow the rules and therefore I am bad"*, because on some level her ability to read emotions was more advanced than the adults around her – which is often the case with children, they are way more intuitive than their parents.

What my Inner Child didn't know or realise at the time was that adults have complex reactions to simple events, because they are always thinking about the series of actions that need to happen in order for them to get everything done before the end of the day: *"Fix the dinner, buy more tomatoes, get a new towel, pick up the dry-cleaning, oh, add antibacterial spray to the list."*

For adults, minor inconveniences can trigger major reactions or strange reactions, mostly because they are not really in tune with their own emotions, since they haven't really connected with their own Inner Child or done any of the healing work.

They weren't taught how to do it or that it's necessary, especially ahead of welcoming a new Soul in their home and raising a child.

This is 100% one of the aspects of parenthood that has been largely missed from education, which has caused a lot of unnecessary childhood trauma globally.

Parents need to evolve their emotional maturity before they welcome new Souls on Earth. Until they do, their children will continue to have to face pain that isn't really theirs – pain that has been given to them through disconnected parenting.

We can talk a lot about pain and what causes us to feel hurt, disappointed, betrayed and even rejected from our own guardians, but the point of pain is to feel it.

There's no workaround. No amount of logic and reasoning will help you when you've been made aware of pain that you're experiencing on an emotional level.

You can try to reason with pain and find the most logical cause as to why you're experiencing it, but the pain won't go away until you actually feel it.

Here's a useful script that you can follow to heal the pain:

1. **FEEL:** Give yourself permission to feel the pain, knowing that you are in the safe space of your own company

2. **CRY:** Give yourself permission to cry as a physical manifestation of feeling the pain and let this become a self-healing ritual for every difficult chapter of your life

3. **LEARN:** Give yourself permission to extract and integrate the lesson from any painful memory that your energy is attached to

4. **LET GO:** Give yourself permission to let go of the energetic connection and use this as an opportunity to rewire your belief system with a new, healthier belief about yourself and your belonging in the world

Reconditioning your subconscious mind starts with your childhood: this is where you obtained your knowledge for the world that has set the parameters for what is possible for you, until you do the inner work to expand it.

It's like setting the course for a voyage and you're the captain of the ship who has a map and a compass.

If the map you were given is an old map, perhaps one that has travelled through many generations before it reached you, it's possible that it is out of date, because the world around us changes pretty fast.

The compass is your heart, or rather, your intuition. For a compass to work, it needs a magnetic field – you are the magnetic field. When your intuition is blocked, your compass needle gets demagnified and its directions become confusing. When you get overwhelmed with emotions, your whole magnetic field gets out of whack and that blocks your compass from doing what it's supposed to do: to guide you.

To revisit an old painful memory and heal it is to open Pandora's box. Your childhood memories link to interconnected thought patterns and a complex belief system that defines your entire existence.

I had to revisit that memory a lot of times until I could go through it from start to finish without crying. I didn't even realise that there was so much pain stored in my body and my whole being that was associated with my childhood.

Intuitive people were once intuitive children. We can hold onto pain as if it's an Olympic game and we're trying to prove our strength to the world. The point of your intuition is to use it to trigger your self-healing journey, so that you can guide other people how to do the same.

Imagine you could replace all the pain that's stored in you with joy! The kind of Light you'll shine in the world with your presence. That's really the purpose of your existence – to collect the pain and heal it, so that you can transform it into love and help others become alchemists, too. This is the ascension journey!

The Gift of **UNCONDITIONAL LOVE**

To unlock the gift of unconditional love is to love yourself INTO being of service to a calling that's greater than you.

How would you recognise your calling? Through your intuition, your inner guidance.

In order to speak directly with your Higher Self, which will guide you further into your calling, you must befriend your Inner Child, so that you can become fluent in the language of intuition and further develop your intuitive abilities. That's how you can access the gift of unconditional love and use it to do good!

Children are the greatest messengers of unconditional love. They arrive into our life to help us access unconditional love when we're ready to ascend and channel more of our potential, but we must be able to love ourselves first or we won't be able to love them the way they deserve, because of our own triggers and innermost wounds that scream for our return within.

The gift of unconditional love is a gift for the whole world, but it operates through us – the tiny humans that hold immeasurable power compared to other beings from the animal kingdom.

We were made to love as our default inner state, so that we can maintain the social structures of Earth at every level of society: at home and at work, in public and in private, with friends and with strangers.

Our ability to love has made it possible to advance humanity beyond the predictable since our authenticity is what makes getting to know each other so exciting.

Whether our ability to love is disabled on purpose (*people intentionally inflict trauma on us to keep us in a state of dissociation*) or accidentally (*we turn off our ability to feel because pain is too unbearable for us to handle based on the level of our emotional maturity*), the journey of self-healing starts with self-awareness.

We must be able to understand where we are today and where we'd like to be next in order to map out the journey and take the necessary first step.

Make no mistake – children arrive into your life not to complete you or to serve you, but to assist you in remembering more of your true nature.

In return, you do the same for them through teaching them of the current state of the world and guiding them how to use their innate abilities, so they can begin to view themselves as the change makers who will one day continue the evolution of Earth.

Heal **YOUR HEART**

Your heart is the most profound tool at your disposal and so you must look after it with great care. If you're ready to restore its natural ability to flow with the Universe, let's do this exercise.

ANSWER the following questions to let empathy lead the way and remove any blockages amidst your heart space:

THE CHOICE TO FEEL YOUR EMOTIONS
(e.g. childhood, parents, siblings, life partner)

"Who's the person that affects your mental health
the most today? Why and in what ways?"

THE ABILITY TO SELF-HEAL
(e.g. abandonment / rejection / trust / betrayal / neglect wound)

"What's your core wound? What's your supporting evidence:
can you find the memories linked to the wound?"

THE GIFT OF UNCONDITIONAL LOVE
(e.g. for yourself, for family, from friends, for colleagues)

"Who needs your unconditional love now the most? Why?
In what ways do YOU need your unconditional love right now?"

Open **YOUR HEART**

The purpose of your heart is to feel everything and experience the full spectrum of emotions. No one is supposed to repress any emotions, but to learn how to recognise them and what they wish to teach us when they appear in our life. Let's learn more about your love language and further open your heart!

Pick one: **EMOTIONS** | **SELF-HEALING** | **UNCONDITIONAL LOVE**

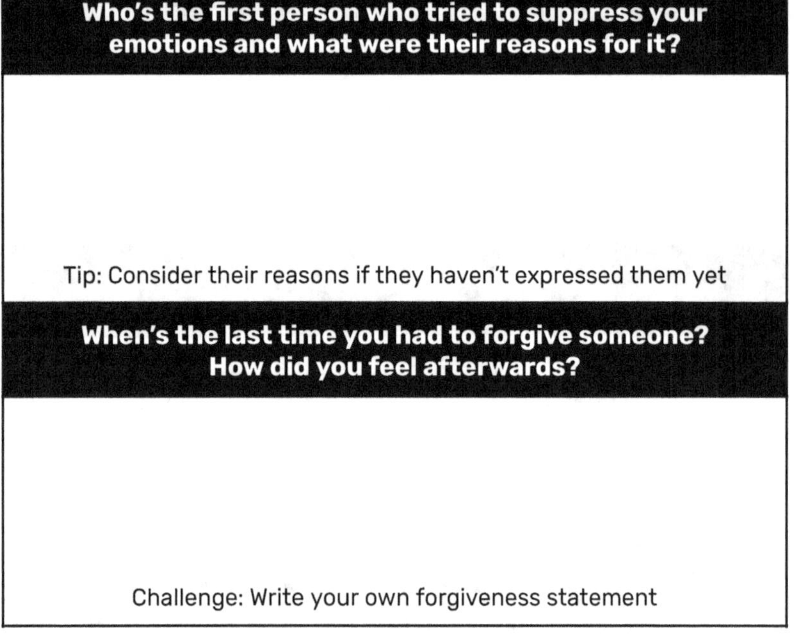

Love can hurt us and it can heal us, too. The HEART is how love operates through us. Remember that you always have the power to alchemise what you've been given and turn it into LOVE.

I think you're now ready to meet your INNER CHILD!

"After all the pain,
you choose to love?"

"Always. There's no force
greater than Love. It can heal any
heart, no matter how wounded,
bitter or disappointed, at any
point of their life journey.
Hearts are made to love!"

Part 5
TO LOVE YOURSELF

The
INNER CHILD

There's no bigger judge for our progress in life than our own inner voice. Not only do we not know how to pace ourselves when it comes to self-love, we are often unable to sit still with our imperfections without trying to change who we are.

What happens when we begin our inner examination is that we focus on the flaws, the cracks, the bruises, the wounds, the aspects of ourselves that are yet to be refined, the losses, the missing parts, the fearsome and impulsive thoughts, the strong desire to be seen, and the consistent choice to hide.

It's a vicious cycle that can defeat even the strongest Spirits, mostly because this cycle doesn't require strength or power to overcome it: it seeks understanding and appreciation.

We think of self-love as a **one-time intervention** that can be completed through a book, a podcast, a show, a conversation, an experience.

It's not.

Self-love is a lifelong process and practise that you choose for yourself. No one has the power to force you to love yourself: not your friends, not your family, not the love of your life.

If you feel incomplete, broken or unworthy on the inside, this will set the tone for every single relationship

in your life as a direct reflection of the relationship you have with yourself.

Remember that your belief system is always working in the background to ensure that there are no glitches in the operational system that you have created for yourself.

Since you are the creator of your inner system, you can change it too. In order to do that, you must become conscious of the script that's running through your subconscious mind, which can be accessed by analysing the patterns in your life.

You have the choice to remain ignorant and to continue to feel insecure, unworthy, insignificant, disempowered and the list goes on.

This is what it means to have free will – you get to decide how you wish to spend your life at all times.

Just like you, other people can choose to remain inconsistent with their behaviour or inconsiderate with their choices, because it suits them. On some level, they like it. It gives them a sense of familiarity and comfort.

Paradoxically, people can affect you to the point of hating and destroying yourself, but they can't really switch on the fountain of self-love that can transform your entire existence. That's a mission for you to accomplish and it starts with choosing better for yourself.

This is where authenticity comes into the picture.

We think of authenticity as **the alchemy of all the best aspects of our identity** that we get to shine out into the world.

It's not.

Authenticity is the absolute representation of all that you are: the good, the bad, the pretty, the ugly, the gifts, the shortcomings. All of it and then some more!

If you choose to hide behind all the best aspects of your personality, this isn't authenticity: it's wearing a mask and filtering your true self as a way to please others or gain their trust, respect, approval (also known as manipulation).

We trust people that are relatable, because we are able to see our strengths and weaknesses in them. Authenticity is fragile, honest, imperfect, vulnerable, exciting. There are levels and layers to authenticity that invite us to explore more of the inner world of people who are brave enough to show their real identity to the world.

It takes honesty to get to know your own authenticity, so that you can share it with the world. Self-love is the practice that allows you to make space for all aspects of you and accept yourself just as you are.

It might take some time, but that's the only way to reconnect with your Inner Child and channel more of your Higher Self: acceptance.

To Accept the **IMPERFECTIONS**

The first hurdle on your self-love journey is making peace with your imperfections.

From the way you look to the way you sound when you express your ideas and how your scars speak of wounds that go deeper than the surface level, you are made to be imperfect.

We are all made to experience many transformations during our short but impactful stay on planet Earth. This could explain why we're made to be imperfect!

We bruise, so that we can appreciate the fragility of our body – the vessel that will be helping us accomplish our purpose. Once we recognise that our actions have an impact on our body, we also understand that we can affect it for the better by taking care of it and applying the right habits into our routine.

We age, so that we can honour the brevity of our existence and live up to our fullest potential with the people around us – consciously, daily, with profound gratitude for the gift of life.

We lose our spark to remember that our spark never really goes away – it's the Inner Light within us that resides with us from the day we're born until the day we die. It's our gift from the Divine that allows us to connect with our Soul mission when we are ready to activate more of our Higher Self.

Until then we are nothing but children – our consciousness fluidly but firmly stuck at the level of immaturity for it is easily influenced by the outside world and not so developed to be able to differentiate between soul tribe members and people who are standing in the way of one's purpose.

In order to recognise who's not aligned with your Soul, *but rather with your Ego*, think about the people who are blocking your growth – the people who encourage you to consume in greater volumes that you can process and ask of you to stay the same, so that you can remain by their side and become witness to their own suffering as validation for their existence on Earth as if their breath is not proof enough they're alive: they need you, too, to parent them or they may not survive, just like children who need constant observation from their guardians.

To see yourself in all of your glory and accept all that you are is the starting point of the next chapter of your life.

To become so immersed into the experience of being alive through your authentic lens and fall in love with the journey of customising your days with pursuits and people that match the genuine thoughts and feelings of your Inner Child: that's the path of self-acceptance and self-actualisation.

And once you accept yourself for all that you are – and all that you can become as a result of all that you've experienced so far – it's time to connect the dots between past, present and future. That is usually when the Universe reveals more about our calling on Earth and invites us on a journey to unlocking more of our potential.

Do you answer the call and accept your calling? That is the question!

If you're brave enough to answer **"Yes!"**, you will proceed to the next lesson.

To Accept the **LIMITATIONS**

The second hurdle on your self-love journey is making peace with your limitations.

The more you connect with your Inner Child, the more you will access your passion for life and every day will be a source of play, inspiration and ideas.

That's when you will face the responsibility to share more of your true authentic self with others along with the realisation that you might not be able to accomplish all that you desire…

Your limitations are attached to the person you'd like to become.

If you wish to be a leader and inspire your community, you will need to focus your time, energy and resources on becoming the best version of yourself when it comes to strategising, networking and being self-disciplined.

If you wish to inspire others with your words, whether you envision yourself as a motivational speaker on a big stage or behind the laptop typing a series of novels, you must embrace a lifestyle of tending to your inner garden, so that you make the best use of the seeds given to you by the Divine.

If you wish to help humanity with your analytical abilities and decide to dedicate your energy and efforts to creating long-lasting changes to the current societal structures, you have to master your time management skills, learn how to say NO to unnecessary distractions and detours, and commit to self-growth unconditionally.

Your limitations are not imposed on you to make you suffer, but to help you uncover what truly excites you to be alive, so that you can spend your lifetime on Earth in the most meaningful ways possible.

Facing your limitations is a necessary step on your journey to reconnecting with your Inner Child, because in the process of living you have probably picked up some dreams, goals and aspirations that aren't even yours: all connected to the people who raised you and helped you become who you are today.

As you let go of the false dreams, incomplete goals and outdated pursuits, take time to practise gratitude for all the Souls who assisted you in getting to this very moment right here and right now.

Some of the people around you will never make it all the way to fully accept their Inner Child and ascend to their Higher Self in their current lifetime, but in the next one they will be able to use your example as the guiding light as they boldly and confidently overcome their previous limitations and unlock new levels of their consciousness.

In the meantime, let's cross the finish line of your self-acceptance marathon together and get your heart-shaped medal to make your victory official!

To Accept Your **INNER CHILD**

The process of reconditioning your subconscious mind and changing your thought patterns is really all about re-parenting your Inner Child in a more loving, caring way that encompasses the imperfections and limitations of the human experience while giving you more permission to fail and try again – as often as every day or until you figure out the formula for happiness that works for you.

To accept your Inner Child is to close a huge chapter of your life that kept bringing you back to the past where all of your unresolved traumas had you under the spell of a number of coping mechanisms.

You are worthy of love. We are all worthy of love. That's the big breaking news!

We turn to coping mechanisms when we are unable to find and feel love for our innermost depths by the people around us and even the world as a whole.

Our inability to process what's happening or the pain from the lack of love guides into a state of trance, also known as dissociation.

We pretend that everything is fine while in the background we continue to detach further from our own true authentic nature – and in doing so abandoning our Inner Child, in the same way our early life guardians and teachers trained us to reject our authenticity in exchange for drops of love.

But there's a well within each of us, *a whole ocean really*, that's a true source of unconditional love.

Sometimes the Universe orchestrates for us to experience extreme neglect, rejection and abandonment, so that we can finally change our perspective and look for the love that we so desperately crave within us, not outside of us.

Our Inner Child can be found there: inside that ocean full of unconditional love, right at the heart of our subconscious mind, strategically positioned to get us to swim to depths we didn't know ourselves to be capable of reaching, so that we can prove to ourselves that we are worthy of all the abundance that's already our birthright.

Meet **YOUR INNER CHILD**

The mission of self-love starts with self-awareness and ends with self-acceptance. What this means is that we are constantly adapting and evolving, which means we are continuously upgrading what makes us who we are. The point of this journey is to do it with your Inner Child!

ANSWER the following questions to get to heart of your Inner Child and integrate more of your experiences:

ACCEPT THE IMPERFECTIONS
(e.g. skills, features, habits, attitude, flaws, appearance)

"Who's the person who has criticised you the most in life? Why?"

ACCEPT THE LIMITATIONS
(e.g. physical, mental, emotional or spiritual blockages)

"What's one area of life where you feel a lot of loss or lack?"

ACCEPT YOUR INNER CHILD
(e.g. work life, home life, society, community, hobbies, goals)

"Where would you focus your attention if you didn't have to worry about money or responsibilities? Why?"

Channel **YOUR INNER CHILD**

Would you believe me if I told you there are aspects of your personality that have been dormant in you since you were a child? Whether your parents ignored elements of your authenticity or society rejected them altogether, it is now safe to open up and embrace your INNER CHILD! Let's do the examination of the innermost parts of your consciousness together:

Pick one: **IMPERFECTIONS | LIMITATIONS | INNER CHILD**

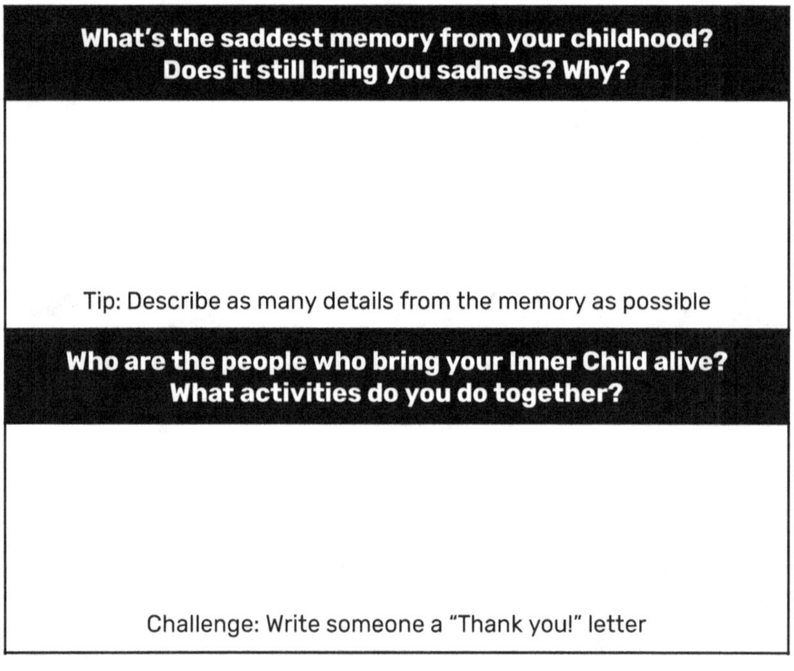

Your INNER CHILD is safe and protected at all times, but it might need more encouragement to come out and play, especially if you've experienced a lot of childhood trauma. Be kind to yourself.

Ready for an adventure? Let's ascend to your HIGHER SELF!

"So it's OK to be imperfect?"

"Absolutely. There's nothing perfect about us beyond the love in our hearts and even that often gets us in trouble. You're perfectly created in the eyes of the Creator!"

The
HIGHER SELF

The first time I met my Higher Self must have been when I was a child. I remember being on my bike and cycling around my grandparents' building when an image flooded my mind.

It was an image of me hosting a TV show – an image that slowly became a whole mini movie, a little bit like the moving images from Harry Potter, only I could enter it and investigate it energetically as if I was an audience member.

What I noticed about this living memory from the future was that I was happy in it, accomplished, and that there was a sense of predetermination in it. This was not merely a snapshot of what's possible, but a glimpse into the future – a timeline outcome that my Higher Self wanted me to preview, so that I can keep it stored in my consciousness in times of doubt.

Another thing I noticed was that while I was confidently asking the guests some really big questions, my Inner Child was puzzled as to how I knew the answers to those questions. It was as if while I was experiencing the memory I was simultaneously the kid who was cycling in my hometown and the woman in front of the camera who was a source of wisdom that I somehow had the inner knowing that I was capable of embodying, but had not yet reached on my evolutionary path.

That's the power of reconnecting with our Higher Self. We don't have to force things in life – relationships, projects, connections, pursuits, agreements. We just need to let life happen.

Children are more connected to their Higher Self because they allow themselves to experience life in a state of play, which is the perfect state to receive guidance from above the Earthly plane.

When we are in a state of play or a state of flow, we are living in unison with the Universe, which prepares us for the unexpected. We are open to it!

A kid doesn't start cycling with a to-do list.

"Oh, I must pick up some bagels, pay my electricity bill and pass through city hall for the documents. Did I take out the trash? Add that to the list, too."

A kid explores.

This is what is asked of us, too – the adults who are ready to establish connection with their Higher Selves and tap into the infinite intelligence of Source, which is really the database of the Universe.

Meditation is not the only way to activate your Higher Self connection and receive inner guidance. Visualisation, praying, setting intentions and engaging in play – these are all great ways for you to strengthen your connection with your Higher Self.

Meditation, however, is an excellent daily practice to help you disconnect from the endless lists of tasks and responsibilities that define your life, so that you can realise you are more than your actions – you are the human being who's worthy of great care and great adventures from the day you arrived here.

You were born to live and experience life on this planet as one of Earth's children.

To Earth, you remain a child, just like a mother sees her offspring as the babies they once were, even after they've got wrinkles on their face and silver streaks in their hair. The way our mothers love to see us happy and prosperous, Earth likes to see us succeed in our pursuits, especially when they bring abundance to her lands and its many inhabitants too.

To Ascend above **THE EGO**

There's no bigger blocker to one's ascension than the Ego, which shouldn't be a surprise to anyone at this point.

The Ego is a protective mechanism that is responsible for shaping our personality and making sure that we don't make a fool of ourselves, which then might have fatal consequences for our social life and ability to fit in.

And there it is! The reason why the Ego blocks our ascension is because it's been designed to support us on **our quest to fit in**, which is part of an outdated modality in our collective evolution.

Essentially, for any of us to be able to reach self-actualisation, we must be brave enough to explore our individuality and break free from the pack (including friends and family) in order for us to truly unlock our authenticity blueprint and embody it. In other words, we must become comfortable standing out and pursuing our destined path regardless of the outside noise.

Oftentimes we are unable to become the person we're destined to be, because of the people around us who have gotten very comfortable with directing our own life as a way to keep us stuck in enmeshed, codependent relationships where no one is truly independent and complete on their own.

This structure actually worked well for our ancestors. They had to live and fight side by side in order to survive. Many cultures around the world still practise the whole multigenerational living under one roof. Sooner or later, it gets messy, complicated and pretty dysfunctional, because the world that we live in today is changing at a speed that our ancestors didn't get to witness.

What's more, every generation is meant to leave a mark in the collective history of humankind, but their biggest contribution should never be to handicap their own heirs by imposing on them their own wounds, dreams and limiting beliefs.

A healthy Ego ensures that you successfully preserve your own individuality while being part of a greater community.

Reconnecting with your Higher Self is not about erasing your Ego, because that would erase the framework for your individuality. Every milestone on your journey so far is important for putting together the story of your life and understanding how best to serve humanity with all of the knowledge you've collected amidst failures, successes and everything in between.

But when the Ego tries to scare you from taking a leap of faith, remember that it's designed to do so as a way to protect your current identity.

Every time that we ascend and level up, we must let go of an aspect of ourselves that is no longer a match to the reality that we're about to experience. This process of shedding is natural and it's part of the self-growth elevation.

The aspects of our identity that can't make it in the next chapter of our life will remain part of our story, our authentic story. This is how your Ego can serve you best – by ensuring that you honour every character flaw and every superpower, because without them you wouldn't have had such a complex, unique path to get you to the present moment as the extraordinary human being that you are.

Failures are some of our greatest teachers for they crack open our hearts to release even more love into the world and embrace the adventure of self-discovery with more determination and appreciation for connecting with others.

Your ascension is about reclaiming your authenticity and channelling more of your potential, but life on Earth has always been and will forever be about co-creating with one another. We are social creatures by design and that is what makes the Earthly journey so exciting – to be able to share our authentic selves with each other as we leave a mark on the world side by side.

In other words, the ascension process of integrating more of your Higher Self as part of your everyday experience of life is 100% a solo mission, because each of us has different lessons to learn and wounds to heal. But at the end of it, we are meant to share who we are with the whole world as we unite with fellow awakened ascended humans on Earth who are aligned with our Soul mission: our true soul tribe.

To Ascend above **THE SYSTEM**

We don't go through all of the healing and the rewiring of our subconscious mind just so that we can feel better in our own skin, even though that's a great benefit.

We accept the call of the Universe, so that we can be of service to others.

In order for us to serve humanity, we must remember who we are and why we're here, otherwise we would be spending our entire life in a series of cycles that reflect back to us our core wounds and false beliefs about our shortcomings.

Many of our parents and grandparents are still stuck in those cycles. Unfortunately, they didn't have the amount of resources that we do to help us break free from all of the conditional programming. While it's true that some of them probably had the chance to heal but chose not to, you shouldn't take their choice personally. If anything, you must remember that it's their choice and not yours.

We all have free will. You have a choice to heal your wounds today, so that you can bring positive change to the generations that will arrive after you. This is how you're serving humanity through being the example in your own family and community.

Once you've gone through your Hero's Journey and recollected all the shattered pieces of your authentic identity, it's time to channel your passion and potential into your very own purpose.

This is the time to think about all the global issues that you can recognise and research what's causing the disharmony in the world. At some point you'll figure out that everything's connected, that education and politics are not really detached, that the food industry and the healthcare industry are intertwined, that there's room for improvement across all aspects of society.

We ascend to become positive change makers. We ascend because we believe in our ability to experience more and to give more. We ascend to dedicate our life to a calling that is greater than our individual goals. We ascend because the thought of not doing so – of giving up on our Inner Child – is too painful to bear.

The system is broken and it needs us to channel our energy and ideas to change it for the better. Make no mistake: those who are currently in power are benefiting greatly from the corrupted structures, which is what makes the choice to ascend and operate in alignment with our Higher Self even more important today.

This is a pivotal time in history for we are connected to one another like never before thanks to technology. Yet if we remain asleep to our own potential and purpose, our ability to affect change in seconds would go to waste. The current rulers of the world are counting on us to remain ignorant, depressed, in a state of dissociation, detached from our calling and disconnected from our peers.

Yet people like me and you are continuing to heal, change, grow, evolve and unite with others – against all odds. Your connection to your Higher Self is divinely guided and divinely protected at all times so long as you continue to choose to ascend.

Use your free will wisely as you ascend above the system and understand that the guidance from within is the one that matters the most.

To Ascend with **YOUR HIGHER SELF**

There are multiple levels to the ascension journey and there isn't a single way to the top. In fact, there are as many routes as you can imagine as there are many "tops" that you can reach!

First, you're ascending to reach your Higher Self, so that you can hear your inner guidance and learn how to interpret it. Then, you begin to take aligned actions that guide you on so many side quests that you hardly even remember who you once were before you started the journey.

Finally, there's just your Higher Self and the old, repressed you is gone. Gone are also the limiting beliefs, the coping mechanisms, the people pleasing, the need for constant validation or approval, the desire to prove yourself, the imposter syndrome and the temptation to overwork yourself as a way to self-sabotage.

To ascend with your Higher Self is to embrace your calling and believe in your multidimensional nature as a way to lead like the leader you always envisioned yourself following – here you are creating that leader within yourself.

From the inside out, I've always listened to my intuition and followed my heart when I had to make decisions in life: the subjects I studied, the jobs I accepted, the people I dated, the books I read, the destinations I explored, the poems I wrote.

From the outside in, I wonder what others have noticed about me – if my actions have been predictable or if I've puzzled some people, if I've been a good friend or an absent one precisely because of my connection to my Higher Self.

I realise that we cannot be everything for everyone at all times, so we must be careful with our choices and the commitments we agree to make.

Maybe I haven't gotten to experience genuine connection with others as my true authentic self, but I have befriended myself in a world that wanted to keep me alienated from my own nature, so I'll take the win.

The question is: are you ready to formulate a plan on how to turn your higher calling into an actual career path on Earth?

Let's do it together!

Ascend to **YOUR HIGHER SELF**

Your Higher Self is your connection to Source – the database of the Universe. It's through your Higher Self that you can access more of life and activate your inner guidance, so that your impact on Earth can reach more people.

ANSWER the following questions to uncover more of your Higher Self and purpose on Earth:

ASCEND ABOVE THE EGO
(e.g. self-image, skills, personality, unique selling points)

"What *really* sets you apart from other people on Earth?"

ASCEND ABOVE THE SYSTEM
(e.g. childhood trauma, corrupted society, bureaucracy)

"How does your upbringing connect to huge COMMUNITY or system issues worldwide?"

ASCEND WITH YOUR HIGHER SELF
(e.g. life purpose, soul mission, childhood dream, leadership goal)

"What was your childhood dream? What's your dream today? Can you find any links between the two?"

Integrate **YOUR HIGHER SELF**

There's no better way to integrate your Higher Self than to trust the guidance from your intuition, which will give you clues as to what people, projects and places are healthy for your evolution. Let's unpack some more of your beliefs as we figure out if there's something blocking your imagination and then release it:

Pick one: **THE EGO | THE SYSTEM | HIGHER CALLING**

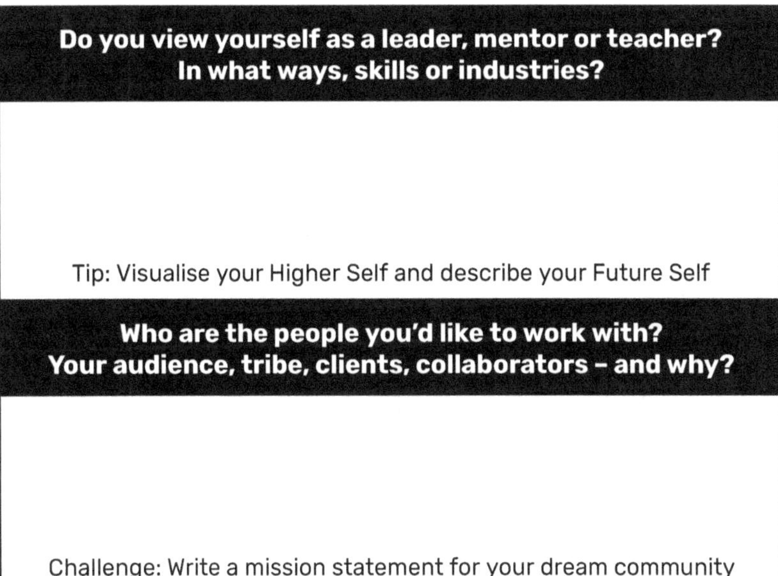

Integrating more of your HIGHER SELF happens when you're ready to align with your purpose and become of service to Earth. Don't be scared to explore the impossible and dream big.

Before we can examine PURPOSE, let's look into PRIDE!

"What's the magic formula?"

"There's no magic formula for reconnecting with your Higher Self and your purpose. Step 1: Make time and space to feel your energetic body. Step 2: Repeat step 1."

Part 6

TO SHARE YOURSELF

PRIDE
to
PEACE

If you met me when I was 20 years old, you would have met a really vibrant, bold, confident and authentic version of myself. I had just moved from my hometown in Bulgaria all the way to Scotland to study journalism at university and my life was a rollercoaster of emotions that introduced me to so many new people and opportunities on a daily basis. It felt like I was finally able to express myself and share my passion for life in a very creative and aligned way: I was truly on top of the world, the top of my personal evolution anyway!

What happened next? I fell in the trap of love. A trap that society prepares us to experience since the day we can form words and differentiate between "Mama" and "Dada".

What's the trap of love?

It's the illusion that you are nobody unless you're in a relationship – that your value has somewhat decreased since no one has claimed you to be *"theirs"*.

Naturally, I also wanted to be someone's muse, so I, too, trusted someone with my heart: a decision that shattered my entire identity and left me recollecting the many pieces of my soul on my own for twice as long as the course of the relationship.

But this chapter isn't about love. This chapter is about overriding your own pride and embracing failure as the teacher that awakens you to greater levels of grace.

My first encounter with love wasn't successful and there are many reasons for it, but one crucial aspect, *which would haunt me in my darkest days*, was the fact that I ignored my spiritual growth the moment I reached the peak of my journey.

My pride destroyed the best aspects of me in ways that no one could have ever impacted me in such a disempowering way.

I knew who I was from the start and that gave me an advantage, yet it never occurred to me that this inner knowing wasn't a given, but rather it was a gateway that opened up for me when I showed up for my spiritual mastery daily.

My self-awareness was built over the course of many years of showing up to read books, research, journal, write down ideas, get to know my preferences, channel my potential in creative pursuits, meet like-minded people and dive deep in meaningful conversations or dance till our feet hurt in the morning hours.

All of that went away, one day at a time.

All the passion I had for life, it vanished from me.

All the ideas that I wanted to share, they escaped me, too, like they didn't want to have anything to do with me anymore.

I can blame my partner for losing my identity, but I'd rather take accountability for the part I played and advise you to never, ever abandon yourself by abandoning your routine and your own personal growth. That's how you fall into the pit of pride and no one can get you out of that pit but yourself.

The Way of **PRIDE**

I said this chapter wouldn't be about love, but there's more to the story that feels important.

The more I wanted to make our relationship work, the more I lost aspects of myself in it – in the void that had formed between us – and the more I faced the animosity in my partner's eyes, as if his heart had no love left for me anymore.

Yet he kept holding my hand and falling asleep beside me: a well-rehearsed ritual to keep the illusion alive. Society had prepared us both to maintain the facade for as long as we could until someone had to wave the white flag and admit defeat.

From wanting to be someone's muse, I became the villain who didn't even deserve an ounce of love for speaking the truth, even though we could both sense it. This relationship wasn't going to work out. There was no happy love left, it seemed, and the love that was left was not enough to save this sinking ship.

We had become morbid lovers who couldn't even find inspiration to channel our aching hearts into songs or poems to share with the world. We were two strangers who kept coming back to one another out of duty. This love story had become so much work that in the end neither of us could hear anything the other was saying, because the love that kept our hearts beating couldn't reach the other. I think it couldn't even reach the surface of our own bodies at the time.

We were numb. Frozen in time. Desperately wanting to bring back the past while being fully aware that nothing could take us there – not even a time machine.

Why did neither of us leave if we weren't happy?

Think about this for a second: why are so many of our parents and grandparents together if they are not happy?

We are the children who diligently followed the example of the generations who came before us. We trusted their guidance and it nearly destroyed us in the same way it killed something in them in order for them to remain together long after their hearts had stopped beating for one another.

I think deep down neither of us wanted to give up on love, but we also didn't want to lose our chance at experiencing life through our own authentic lens. At the time it sucked, because young people should be celebrating – not looking for ways to numb their heart, since the pain of love feels too much to bear.

I guess that's the way of pride: you feel like you can't simply abandon the image of the person you've presented yourself to be, even when you know that this isn't who you are and that what you're doing is no longer making you happy.

No amount of physical connection could have brought us closer, because in our hearts we were miles apart – each seeking a way to self-actualise without the other but never admitting that even to our own Self.

Don't let pride destroy your chances at living wholeheartedly as your true self.

Have you ever lost yourself in a relationship? In a friendship? At work? It's OK.

We all get lost in life from time to time. It's how we return back home that matters and the choice to learn from our mistakes can transform our entire existence.

Where's home? Everything and everyone that brings peace to your Soul, but above all the space you provide for your Inner Child to feel safe to come out and play with others.

The Way of **PEACE**

"You must not love me. You never fight with me."

These were actual words I heard from my partner who confused my aversion to conflict for lack of love. Or perhaps it was something like *"I wish you fought more with me, this would have shown me you cared about us – about me."*

I grew up around people who screamed and communicated their confusion through loudness that suffocated every atom of my being. The last thing I want to do is bring more chaos and anger into the world through conflict!

I am a Messenger of Peace, an Agent of Balance, and one of the Earth Angels who are on a mission to protect the sacred lands of our ancestors that have given us life, hope, faith, abundance and natural riches beyond measure from the Dark Ages until today.

My journey to peace has always been driven by an inner desire for self-expression that allowed everyone around me to be seen as well. Maybe over the years I've tried to make way for others to shine as I took a step back, because I had experienced firsthand what it is like to not be acknowledged for all that you are. Some mistook my kindness or silence for weakness. Others even made fun of it.

But my declaration for peace remains. If you wish to enter my life, you cannot do so unless you are willing to protect my peace and fight against unnecessary conflict.

I know a lot of people who live for the drama, the gossip, the plot twists – I am not one of them. The bridges I've burned were connected to people who brought their inner conflicts into my world and I have no regrets for separating myself from their inner wars.

The way of peace is often understood at a later age when one has experienced the pain of the world and made a promise to not contribute further to its fearful agenda. I made that promise when I was still a child, perhaps even in the womb of my mother as my Soul was anticipating its rebirth as myself – Stella.

My wish for the world is for everyone to experience peace, so that they never crave the dysregulation of their nervous system to define their offspring, too.

We have sacrificed too much already by being in this fight-or-flight state from dusk to dawn, permanently worried about something or someone, desperately praying to God for help but never actually listening to what the Creator has to say to guide us.

The guidance is always available. You only need to choose the way of peace and you will be able to access it. This will allow you to shift your whole life for the better and shift the lives of the generations that are yet to arrive, too.

From **PRIDE** to **PEACE**

True power comes from peace. It does not come from being right, but from being in alignment with the Truth and being honest with yourself and the rest of the world.

Make no mistake: pride might feel like a mission for your Mind or your Heart, but it has everything to do with your Soul. There are battles you are overcoming on a spiritual level every time you are able to make it all the way from pride to peace.

Pride is the language of the Ego. Peace is the language of the Soul.

There's healthy pride in the same way there's healthy Ego. But chaos is never the right way to live your life – only peace.

Nietzsche once wrote, *"One must still have chaos in oneself to be able to give birth to a dancing star."*

If you investigate Nietzsche's life path, you'll discover that he was a troubled Soul with many silent battles that defined his work in multiple ways. Often referred to as one of the most brilliant minds to live on Earth, Nietzsche is an example of the wounded masculine Ego that had plenty of encounters with Pride and Peace, without ever fully befriending and committing to either.

But this is your story, your trauma, your wounds, your Inner Child, your Higher Self!

How would you like to spend the rest of your life? Would you like to be a Messenger of Peace and Hope for the next generations? Do you think you have what it takes to face Pride and clear your name as a Peace Maker through choosing to pave your own path instead of following society's expectations?

Your choices today will dictate the storyline of your future.

The way you decide to share yourself will set a precedent for the way others treat your Heart, explore your Mind and connect with your Soul.

Remember that you can always start again – if anything, you're encouraged to start as many times as you'd like in order to find the perfect formula for authentic self-expression that will allow you to channel more of your potential and invest your energy in building some amazing adventures with the people you love.

You're the masterpiece and the Creator. Get the alchemical balance between pride and peace right and you might just change the whole world!

Override **PRIDE**

One of the most famous literary masterpieces is titled *'Pride and Prejudice'*. To this day, these two modalities of our inner wiring continue to prevent us from truly sharing ourselves authentically and connecting meaningfully with others. Let's examine your pride together!

Complete the following sentences to release the blockages that may have impacted your mindset, attitude and expression:

PRIDE IN RELATIONSHIPS
(e.g. expectations, habits, attitude, core beliefs)

"I would never date or befriend someone who…"

PRIDE IN SOCIETY
(e.g. collective thinking, corrupted industries, generational patterns)

"If I had a magic wand, I'd fix this society issue: …"

PRIDE IN YOUR SELF-EXPRESSION
(e.g. confidence, milestones, attributes, achievements)

"One thing I won't shut up about is… BECAUSE… "

Embrace **PEACE**

The journey from PRIDE to PEACE is a long one, but it's worth embarking on it, because in it you will discover many hidden talents and obscured attitude pathways that will help you channel your potential with more ease.

Let's take a step towards restoring your inner balance together!

Pick one: **RELATIONSHIPS | SOCIETY | SELF-EXPRESSION**

Who are the people that allow you to be yourself without having to explain or defend yourself?

Think about: What qualities or values do they share in common?

What did the relationship between your parents look like when you were growing up? Was there conflict or peace?

Challenge. Write a letter to your parents from your 5-Year-Old Self POV

A healthy sense of Self is necessary to be able to set boundaries and express who we are, so long as PRIDE doesn't replace and suffocate our inner PEACE altogether.

Ready for the final chapter? Let's dive into your PURPOSE!

"What's it like at the top?"

PURPOSE

to

PLAN

In the School of Life, everyone has a purpose and a unique learning path that helps you get prepared for accomplishing your soul mission.

When I was a teenager, I thought I was here to be a dancer. I loved being in charge of the choreography as I watched us translate the vibrations of the music into dance moves as a team.

Then I discovered the power of storytelling and that I had the ability to choreograph how the words danced on the blank piece of paper as they created a whole symphony that would be experienced in the theatre hall of your mind.

While the passion for dancing faded over the years, my love for storytelling only grew stronger and so I decided to pursue it as a career.

I won my first literary competition when I was still in high school and it set a course for my life that impacted every consequent decision. Interestingly enough, I didn't go to hundreds of competitions afterwards, but I remember the name of the first one I won: *"The Magic of Words".*

What changed within me was the inner knowing that I was meant to write because my words had a healing effect on the world and soon enough there was a book that wanted to be channelled through me.

In the past year I've undergone the most intense spiritual awakening and ascension that have given me further instructions about my purpose and how I am to use my gifts, which have actually multiplied in the process of trusting the Universe.

This isn't the book I wanted to write. This is a gift from the Divine. And the Dragons!

For the longest time I thought my purpose was to write a book about happiness, but I kept running into obstacles, delays, detours and difficulties putting everything I had learned about joy into words. It took me a while to figure out that I wasn't actually happy and then some more time to understand why that was…

My creative quest was about diving deep into the ocean of my subconscious mind to research pain and how it affects the psyche of humans, in particular the connection with our Inner Child.

So one might say that every single heartache I've experienced on my journey was simply another module of the research my Soul volunteered to compete to advance the database of the Universe: Source.

A partner who couldn't love me unconditionally. Friends who couldn't see me in all of my authenticity. Colleagues who competed with my energetic power instead of harnessing it to co-create with me. Strangers who took my positivity as a personal attack on their choice to be miserable.

All of my experiences collected in the span of 31 years led me to complete my research as to how pain, *one of the most misunderstood emotions*, holds great information about our belonging in the world and what truly matters to us when it comes to sharing our authenticity.

I started my storytelling quest with the goal to write a book about happiness, but ended up creating a healing guide about overcoming pain and how to alchemise it into purpose.

The Dragons are happy, because they know a thing or two about pain and having their freedom limited as they often end up put in bondage across the many stories told around the world. They are excited to meet the next wave of creative thinkers who are willing to work with them to design new storylines full of magic, adventures and love. Yes, representation matters!

The Divine is even happier, because if you've made it this far into the book, this means that you are ready to unlock more information about your own calling on Earth and how you can be of service to others. You've already taken the journey to healing and ascending, now it's time to align with your purpose.

Your purpose is the combination of your life experiences and your Soul's unique learning path that ensures its continued evolution.

There's no shortcut to discovering your purpose in the same way there are no shortcuts to accomplishing it!

There's an abundance of guidance along the way and plenty of resources to get you to uncover and share more of your brilliant insights, so that you can transform your potential into actual progress during your lifetime on Earth.

No detail of your story so far is too small to ignore, yet don't try to fit your whole identity into the framework of what's familiar: you are capable of so much more and destined to experience so much more so long as you choose to grow and continue to advance yourself.

The rest of your life story begins at this very moment. You are here to experiment, connect and channel your energy into the present moment as you envision tomorrow's world. Let's see what your next breakthrough looks like!

The Discovery of **YOUR PURPOSE**

There were several pivotal moments on my healing journey that cracked open the protective shell around my identity that preserved my authenticity intact, but closed off for many years.

I had forgotten aspects of who I truly was and adopted features of those around me in my attempt to fit in as I was licking my wounds in private.

To this day, very few people know the depths of my pain, but I'd rather let people know about my purpose, because it feels more important in today's world.

Yes, pain is all around us, because the destruction of natural resources and human lives is still happening globally, but when one finds their purpose, their life becomes filled with meaning, which is the ultimate antidote to pain.

What gives us meaning also allows us to channel our love. Our purpose is designed to guide us how to tap into the joy of giving and sharing ourselves, so that we can offer our love in a way that can impact thousands of people.

To say I discovered my purpose accidentally would be a lie, but it wouldn't be far from the truth either.

In my wildest dreams I would not have considered the possibility of assisting people interpret their authenticity blueprint using astrology and numerology. This knowledge that appears to be inherent for my Soul was brought to my attention during my ascension, as if it was buried deep inside of me to be discovered exactly when I am ready to make use of it for the good of society.

There were some people who came on my path who wanted to steal that knowledge from me even before I knew it existed in me.

That's the thing with thieves and narcissists – they always talk too much.

Let people show you who they are through the simple act of listening and they will disclose everything. They will tell you lies, illusions, confessions of their grandiose Ego, bold plans, false memories, twisted fantasies, and even the truth about who they really are. This chapter is not about them, it's about you.

Here's how you can learn more about your purpose and how I learned more about mine:

1. **YOUR LIFE PATH** is determined based on the total number of your name[2]. Take the first letter of each of your names and write them down. Each letter equals a number – the total (single-digit) number is your life path. This is numerology in action! Every name gives you clues about your purpose, too.

2. **YOUR HIGHER SELF** is determined by your Sun Sign: this is the energy that you must embody to release more of your potential during your lifetime. The house in which your Sun Sign is placed will guide you where to focus your research and efforts. Your pre-existing identity, which you're here to use to guide others, is your Moon Sign.

3. **YOUR SOUL PURPOSE** can be found in your North Node. This is your current learning path, which will allow you to accomplish what you came here to do: your soul mission. The knowledge you've gathered so far, or the research you have completed, can be found in your South Node.

---

[2] **EARTH INSTRUCTIONS:** Every letter equals a number. Learn more about my method at **stellayann.com/lightworkers**

Please bear in mind that the discovery of your purpose marks the beginning of the next chapter of your life. The people who were with you in the previous chapters might not be able to make it with you onto the next one.

This is an important detail, because you have to make peace with detaching from their energies when the time comes. More often than not, **we ascend, so that we can align with our purpose**, which brings forward brand new people, places, opportunities and horizons for us to explore.

The ascension journey is a solo mission, just like your healing journey. On the other side, however, you will discover a whole bunch of people who have been waiting to meet you to start co-creating with you, so you can re-imagine Earth together.

The Activation of **YOUR PURPOSE**

There are many ways that you can be of service to Mother Earth and its children – your brothers and sisters – during your lifetime.

You can pursue a career path and commit to a social calling that's connected to your personal experience on Earth. Perhaps your own mother suffered from a disease that brought tremendous pain and heartache in the family. Maybe you lost a sibling in an awful accident that could have been prevented if there were different societal structures in place in your community. It's entirely possible that you inherited a business from your father and now it's your turn to continue to develop the family legacy.

These are all examples of a social calling that's connected to what you have personally experienced, which has affected how you view the world and what brings you meaning at the level of your heart.

There's a level that goes deeper – the level of your Soul or Higher Self. That's where you'll discover your higher calling and activate something much larger than just yourself or even your family as a whole: the Divine Plan.

The Divine Plan is a master plan that is far too complex for anyone to truly grasp it, which is why it arrives in bits and pieces channelled through multiple messengers on Earth. It is a plan that brings change on a global level through frameworks that allow for societal mutations for generations to come that encompass different cultures, histories and customs: a plan that thrives on authenticity.

In order for you to understand your higher calling and align with your higher purpose, you will 100% activate dormant spiritual gifts that might be referred to as intuitive skills or psychic abilities. This is the only way for you to establish connection with the Divine and your Spirit Team, so that you can continuously receive guidance as to the part that you're meant to play in the accomplishment of this Divine Plan.

The more you begin to work with your Higher Self, the more you'll discover two modalities within you:

1. **The Inner Leader** who is guided by the passion of your Inner Child and the skills you have developed during your lifetime.

2. **The Higher Leader** who is guided by the expansiveness of your Higher Self and the insights that you have collected during the span of your existence across multiple lifetimes, timelines, dimensions and galaxies.

The Inner Leader is refined and communicated through the frameworks of your Ego, which allows you to retain a consistent narrative of your authentic story as you add new chapters and plot developments to it.

The Higher Leader is channelled when guidance needs to be received or when you are seeking answers that cannot be answered by the people or resources around you.

Your Higher Self has greater capabilities than your Inner Child and Ego combined, but it cannot exist on its own, because you will lose your footing in life – you will not be able to ground what it is that you're here to do in a way that's actionable and achievable.

You must retain your human nature as much as possible for this is the way of life on Earth. We are here to experience what it means to be human and how much we can advance that definition without losing our human features and our ability to love each other with all of our imperfections and limitations!

We discover our Higher Self, so that we can recognise one another for the greatness of our Souls, while we continue to pour our love into appreciating our authenticity defined by many flaws, wounds and traumas – collective and individual.

The activation of your purpose will activate the magic in your life, which is what makes the spiritual ascension journey so exciting. But understand that your gifts are only getting activated, so that you can use them to accomplish your purpose.

You might notice that your gifts get increased or decreased depending on what you need to achieve at present, since you might be using different psychic or spiritual abilities in different chapters of your life.

While it's true that there's only one of you, it's your commitment to your purpose that makes you a loyal servant of the Divine. As long as you choose to be of service to humanity, you will be trusted with guidance, gifts and glory in unmeasurable amounts for that is the way of abundance: it showers those who are worthy to receive it based on the pureness of their hearts.

From **PURPOSE** to **PLAN**

I've talked about the Divine Plan, but there's another plan that you must honour. Your action plan!

Whether you like to write things down using pen and paper or you prefer to collect your goals and dreams on a vision board with the help of AI-powered softwares, it's important to get started on forming your plan as soon as you begin to receive your breakthroughs in the form of ideas and seeds of inspiration.

The vision for the future might be clear, but how you get there is open to interpretation and depends entirely on you and this is why there will be aspects of the journey that remain open to interpretation. You will continuously receive guidance in times of need, but you must become comfortable with customising your adventure by infusing it with your authenticity.

The execution of your purpose is the story that will remain long after you're gone: a story that will inspire generations of young change makers who are embracing their role in the Divine Plan.

A perfect plan without action is just a plan. In order to accomplish your purpose, you must couple your ability to perceive the vision for the future with action on a daily basis.

You are the Change Maker you've been waiting for. You are the Leader, the Teacher, the Mentor, the Healer, the One who is brave enough to pave the way for others!

Don't let the failures of the past dictate the outcome of your future efforts.

Don't let the pain of your previous encounters with Love discourage you from trusting others and allowing them to see your true authentic self.

You are a child of the Divine and a source of Love, just like everyone else on Earth.

Let your energetic body awaken and ascend to new heights as you consistently practise embodying more Love – and Light – as part of your Higher Self integration.

When in doubt, remember that everything is connected. On the other side of Shame is Ascension, Guilt is connected to Acceptance, Grief wants to bring Awareness, Fear is showing up to get you to analyse it and let it go. Anger? That's your Soul's energy channelled inwards – let it flow openly and you will experience the creative intelligence of the Universe.

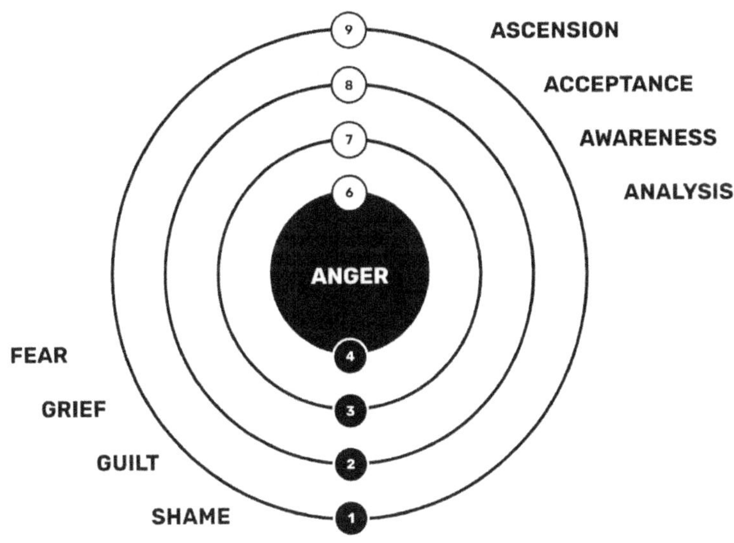

On the other end of suppressing your emotions, there's the freedom to be yourself in all of your authenticity as the Inner Child, the Ego and your Higher Self.

Unlock **YOUR PURPOSE**

One of my favourite quotes is by Mark Twain: *"The two most important days in your life are the day you are born and the day you find out why."*[3]

Complete the following sentences to find your way back to your purpose with the guidance of your INNER CHILD:

THE DISCOVERY OF YOUR PURPOSE
(e.g. favourite hobbies, topics, destinations, jobs, tasks)

"I would work for free if I had the chance to…"

THE ACTIVATION OF YOUR PURPOSE
(e.g. career progression, degree subjects, qualifications)

"I would go back to university to study…"

FROM PURPOSE TO PLAN
(e.g. impressive achievements, rare talents, insanely good skills)

"One skill people always praise me for is my ability to…"

---

[3] **SOUL PURPOSE DISCOVERY:** Get 50% off from our first call with promo code DRAGONSOUL. Learn more at **stellayann.com/lightworkers**

Turn **PURPOSE** into **PLAN**

Understanding your strengths and superpowers has everything to do with understanding how to use them for the betterment of society and all of humanity. The first step is to unlock your authenticity blueprint – the second one is to apply the knowledge into action. Let's start with some defining questions that will help you build a clearer vision for your aligned lifestyle!

Pick one: **PURPOSE DISCOVERY | ACTIVATION | EXECUTION**

> **What are skills and gifts you'd like to use daily to help others and continue to channel your own potential?**
>
> Tip: Consider skills and gifts you're yet to develop and master, too
>
> **What industries or global causes would you like to support with your work?**
>
> Challenge: Visualise your last day on Earth. What's your impact?

The day you choose to be of service to humanity is the day you become an Earth Ambassador: someone who looks after the wellbeing of all living beings today, tomorrow and for many generations to come afterwards. Thank you for believing in your ability to be A CHANGE MAKER – I believe in you too!

This marks the end of our healing journey together. May we meet again soon. I know the Dragons have more messages to channel. In the meantime, may the Love of the Most High be with you!

"How would you like
to be remembered?"

"As a Change Maker."

THE SELF-LOVE JOURNEY

The most important relationship in your life is the one with yourself, because it sets the tone for every single connection that you form, build and strengthen.

Bring more compassion in your life with **A 3-WEEK COURSE** to grounding your root chakra: the first energy centre in the body. This is a guided practical course that can be taken in 2 different ways – with or without coaching.

Self-love is the key to unlocking more of your potential and uncovering your most authentic self. There's a Leader, a Teacher, a Healer, a Mentor, a Guiding Light within you that can only be awakened through self-love. Let's unlock it together!

www.stellayann.com/selflove

About the Author
STELLA YANN

A storyteller on a mission to bring spirituality down to Earth and create a more authentic world filled with joy. As a Brand Storyteller, Stella helps leaders unlock their soul purpose and create positive change in the world with their authentic story as a small business or motivated individual.

For her network, she is an Authenticity Alchemist who can tap into other people's inner child and guide them back to their passion. For her Spirit Team and as part of her higher calling, Stella is a Lightworker on a mission to awaken New Earth Leaders worldwide.

Born and raised by the Black Sea, Stella has found a second home in the UK. Her Soul, however, originates from a place far away from Earth. In the meantime, she's here as an intergalactic traveller who's curious to meet fellow Lightworkers and people who are excited about restoring our beloved planet to a new Golden Age.

ALCHEMY Notes:

AIR bends your mindset. How has your mindset about self-love, Inner Child, Higher Self, purpose and success shifted after reading this book?

FIRE fuels your passion. Have you rediscovered old passion projects or childhood dreams that you're feeling called to work on?

WATER awakens your heart. Who are the people you want to share this book with and why? What qualities or interests do you have in common?

EARTH grounds your actions. What are 5 habits you can't wait to start or strengthen in the next 30 days?

Thank you for joining me
on this healing adventure
and embarking on your
own **HERO**'s journey
to reclaim your power.

You're now an Alchemist.